COZUMEL

COZUMEL

THE COMPLETE GUIDE II

Patricia A. Holt

"Cozumel The Complete Guide II," by Patricia A. Holt. ISBN 978-1-60264-345-1.

Published 2011 by Cozumel the Complete Guide, Calle 17 #550 Esq FCO Mujica Indenpendencia, Cozumel, Q. Roo, Mexico 77664☐2011, Patricia A. Holt. All rights reserved. No part of this publication may be reproduced, stored in a retrieval system, or transmitted in any form or by any means, electronic, mechanical, recording or otherwise, without the prior written permission of Patricia A. Holt.

Manufactured in Merida, Mexico.

TABLE OF CONTENTS

Dear Readers:

If you are reading this book, then I will assume that you are either planning or dreaming of a vacation in Cozumel. You will not regret this decision, I promise.

I was a frequent visitor to Cozumel for 11 years before I made the big move. In August of 2007 I made Cozumel my home. Many people begin to dream of moving here after only one visit. Cozumel is a wonderful place both to live and to visit.

The one thing I was unable to find during the first nine years of visits was a comprehensive guide about Cozumel. None existed, until November 2005 when the first copy of "Cozumel the Complete Guide" was published. Yes I found a few books that would have one or two chapters pertaining to Cozumel, such as Frommer's, and an Idiot's Guide to Mexico's Beaches, but nothing solely dedicated to this beautiful island, and in depth.

A lot has changed since I wrote that guide and it is way past time for an update. I hope that you will enjoy and make much use of this new edition and the coupons we have provided. Although there are a couple of guidebook type maps, a dive guide, and another privately published and sold guidebook on the market today, none are as comprehensive in their information about Cozumel. Many of them are a perfect complement when purchased in addition to "Cozumel the Complete Guide II".

Not everyone vacations the same way. This book can be used by the backpacker on a shoestring budget or by a family on the vacation of a lifetime. No matter where your vacation budget falls, this guide will be a welcome asset in planning your trip. Be sure to make use of our coupons in the back.

NOTE: *The tourist and travel industry is a constantly changing market. The information and prices contained within may vary due to these changes. Where Mexican Pesos are quoted it will say mp or MP.*

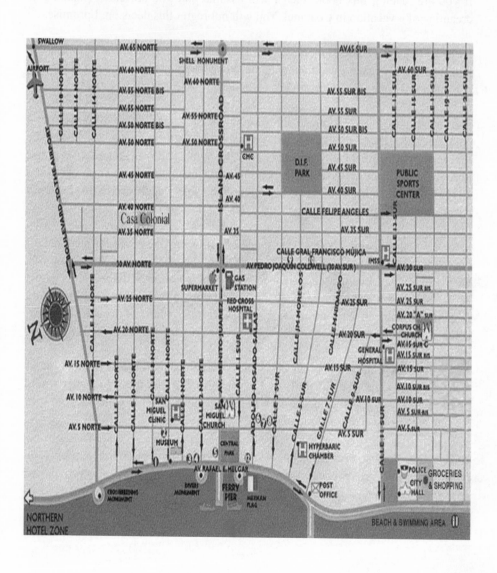

INTRODUCTION TO COZUMEL

BIENVENIDO AL PARAISO, or in English, WELCOME TO PARADISE

Settled by the ancient Mayans over two thousand years ago, the Mayan name for Cozumel is "Ah Cuzamil Petén", which translates to Island of the Swallows. The island was a shrine to Ixchel, the Mayan goddess of fertility. Mayan women from the mainland were expected to make at least one trip in their life to worship here.

In 1518, the Spanish explorer Juan de Grijalva arrived to the coast of the island on Holy Cross Day (May 3rd), named this land as "Isla de la Santa Cruz" and proclaimed the land as property of the Doña Johanna and Don Carlos Kings of Spain. Hernán Cortés arrived on Cozumel in 1519. A year later, he started his conquest of Mexico (and Belize). Initially, there were no large-scale confrontations between the Indians and the Spaniards on the island. By 1524, the conquest was complete. The Mayan ruler of Cozumel accepted their domination peacefully. The conquistador proceeded to destroy many of the Mayan temples. At the same time, an outbreak of smallpox killed thousands. By the time, Cortés left Cozumel, the ancient civilization lie in ruins. By 1570 most of the Maya population were dead, murdered by the Conquistadors or killed off by disease. By 1600 Cozumel was abandoned.

During the early 17th Century pirates had discovered Cozumel. Henry Morgan used this island hide-away between 1658 and 1688. The tales about Jean Lafitte, who attacked the many ships passing near Cozumel between 1814 and 1821, say he hid from his pursuers in the safe harbors of the Passion Island. Cozumel remained deserted until 1847, when 20 families fleeing the Spanish backlash over the Maya rebellion during the War of the Castes settled on the island and founded El Cedral. Many of their descendants are still living on the island. Cozumel soon settled into a forgotten island community.

Cozumel also has a place in the history of chewing gum. In the late 1800s, a Mexican general, Antonio Lopez de Santa sent a shipment of chicle to the United States after observing the natives of Mexico and Central America chewing sap from the zapote tree. He gave it to Thomas Adam who tried to invent rubber but instead

9

invented chewing gum. When Frank and Henry Fleer coated their gum with sugar and called it «Chiclets», chewing gum became the most popular candy in America and the demand for chicle reached an all-time high. Locals harvested chicle sap from the Manilkara chicle tree on the island (Cozumel was a port of call on the chicle export route). The natural gum was sugar-coated in America and turned into the now famous Chiclets. Eventually a synthetic chewing gum was invented and the need for chicle faded, as did Cozumel's major industry.

Cozumel's economy remained strong with the building of a US air base during WWII. American military diving teams trained in the waters of Cozumel for their Pacific operations. Unfortunately, in the process they dismantled most of the Maya ruins without realizing what they were destroying. When the US military departed, the island fell into an economic slump and many of its people moved away. All those who stayed fished for a livelihood.

In the 1950s Cozumel became a resort town for rich Yucatecans who came to the island to fish, sunbathe and relax. A display in the Cozumel Island Museum outlines the history of the families who founded the modern Cozumel and the very first luxury hotels.

In 1961 Jacques Cousteau discovered the wonders of diving in Cozumel, and declared it one of the greatest dive areas of the world. After that, Cozumel's tourist industry took off and continues to grow larger every year. Cozumel now draws thousands of visitors every day. Known for its world famous dive sites and beautiful white beaches, it is located on the second largest barrier reef system in the world. The Great Mayan Barrier Reef extends from the northern Yucatan to the Honduras.

Cozumel is a popular cruise ship port with as many as 11 ships docking each day. There is much more than diving on this small island, which measures twenty-eight miles long and ten miles wide. There is much to see and do here. Enjoy water sports, shopping, exploring, or just plain relaxing on the beach with a cold drink and a good book.

One need not be a diver to enjoy what Cozumel has to offer, or to appreciate the warmth and hospitality of the local residents, some of who are direct descendants of the original Mayans. Sit in the Plaza on a balmy Sunday evening, listen to the music, dance, and hand out candy to the many young children. You will be rewarded with some of the biggest and brightest smiles you have ever seen.
One visit to Cozumel, and I promise you it will not be your last. On behalf of my friends and the local community of Cozumel, WELCOME!

COZUMEL CALENDAR

JANUARY

New Year's Day (January 1): This is a national holiday, but most celebrating is done New Year's Eve. Most Mexicans celebrate New Year's Eve by having a late-night dinner with their families. Those who want to party generally go out afterwards.

Three Kings Day (January 6): Christmas continues on through Epiphany, which is called Dia de Los Reyes or Three Kings Day and to Mexican children is much more important than December 25. On the eve of Kings Day, the children leave their shoes out in the hopes that they will wake up to find them filled with toys and other treasures, just as the magi came bearing gifts for the newborn infant so long ago.

Children and adults gather on January 6 to partake of a traditional treat called Rosca de Reyes or kings' bread, which is crown-shaped sweet bread decorated with "jewels" of candied fruit. Tiny plastic baby Jesus figures are hidden in the dough before baking and custom dictates that whoever gets a piece of bread containing a baby is responsible to host another party on Candlemas, February 2.

FEBRUARY

Día de la Candelaria (February 2): In Mexico Día de la Candelaria is a follow-up to the festivities of King's Day on January 6th, when children receive gifts and families and friends break bread together, specifically Rosca de Reyes, special sweet bread with figurines hidden inside. The person (or people) who received the figurines on Kings Day is supposed to host the party on Candlemas Day.

Constitution Day (February 2): A national public holiday to commemorate the constitution of 1917 that was put in place by Venustiano Carranza followingthe Mexican Revolution. There are and ceremonies commemorating this national holiday.

Carnaval: Carnaval takes place the week before Ash Wednesday (dates vary from year to year). Cozumel is home to one of the most popular Carnaval celebrations in the Mexican Caribbean. It happens at the peak of high season when the weather is at its finest. It is so much fun to see the magnificent costumes, dancing and awesome floats during the parades of Cozumel. From the room of your Cozumel Hotel you may hear a mixture of calypso, reggae, flamingo and pop music, each distinct but blending into the cultural mix that is Cozumel.

Valentine's Day - Día del Amor y Amistad (February 14): In Mexico this day is to celebrate friendship, as well as love. Friends and lovers exchange cards, gifts or flowers.

Flag Day - Día de la Bandera (February 24): Children get the day off and banks and government offices are closed. Civic ceremonies take place to honor the tri-color, Mexico's flag.

MARCH

Holy Week - Semana Santa (Dates vary from year to year): Festivities take place during the week leading up to Easter, but many people have the following week off as well, stretching it out to a two week holiday. Religious processions and plays re-enacting the Passion of Christ are commonly held, but for many Mexicans this is a favorite time to hit the beach. It's high season for travel; so if you plan to be in Mexico during. Holy Week, make hotel reservations well in advance.

Benito Juarez' Birthday - Natalicio de Benito Juarez (March 21): One of Mexico's most beloved leaders, sometimes referred to as the "Mexican Abraham Lincoln," Benito Juarez went from being a poor Zapotec Indian to become Mexico's first (and only) native president. He made education free and mandatory and brought in the separation between church and state. His birthday is celebrated as a national public holiday.

13

Spring Equinox (Late March): Visitors come to the main temple at Chichen Itza to see the descent of the serpent Kukulkan. History has it that the Maya constructed the temple in a way that during equinox a beam of sunlight creates a shadow moving down towards earth resembling a slithering snake. This occurrence is supposed to bring out a good harvest.

APRIL

Feria del Cedral (varies year to year April or May): Takes place at the ancient Mayan settlement of El Cedral, locals commemorate the Day of the Holy Cross (Día de la Santa Cruz) with cattle exhibitions, rodeos and bullfights. Also remembered is the arrival of the island's 11 founding families, who escaped to Cozumel from the mainland during The Caste War (La Guerra de Castas) in 1848.

International Sport Fishing Rodeo Tournament (dates vary): This international sport-fishing tournament is a good time for you avid fishermen. It brings together competitors from around the world to fish for dorado, marlin, tuna, sierra and other game fish.

MAY

Cozumel's International Billfish Tournament (dates vary): Competitors from around the world compete in Cozumel's Gulf waters. This is a "catch and release" Tournament.

Dia del Trabajo - Labor Day (May 1): This is a national public holiday in Mexico. There are political and labor union marches and official speeches. Schools, banks and government offices are closed.

Cinco de Mayo (May 5): This is a national holiday commemorating Mexico's defeat of the French in the Battle of Puebla in 1862.

Dia de la Madre - Mother's Day (May 10): Mother's Day is always celebrated on May 10th in Mexico, regardless of the day of the week (unlike in the U.S. where it is celebrated on the second Sunday in May).
Mothers are held in very high esteem in Mexican culture and on this day they are celebrated in style.

JUNE

Father's Day - Día del Padre (June second Sunday): Now it is Dad's turn to be treated like royalty.

SEPTEMBER

Independence Day - Día de la Independencia (September 16): Viva Mexico! Mexico celebrates its independence from Spain in 1821. The celebrating actually begins the evening prior with fireworks and partying. This national celebration is observed here in Cozumel with a grand fireworks display in front of the Municipal Building on Raphael Melgar. There will be countless types of local cuisine in the nearby food court as well as games and rides for the kids.

Autumn Equinox (Late September): Visitors come to the main temple at Chichen Itza to see the descent of the serpent Kukulkan. History has it that the Maya constructed the temple in a way that during an equinox a beam of sunlight creates a shadow moving down towards earth resembling a slithering snake. This occurrence is supposed to bring out a good harvest.

Feast of San Miguel (September 29): This feast day honoring the patron saint of Cozumel's largest town is celebrated in September with a mix of religious and popular traditions.

OCTOBER

Halloween (October 31): This American holiday is slowly catching on in Cozumel. On my last Halloween we had about 15 children come to our door and yell "trick or treat", usually with a bit of parental coaxing.

NOVEMBER

Dia de Los Muertos—Day of the Dead (November 2): More than 500 years ago, when the Spanish conquistadors landed in what is now Mexico, they encountered natives practicing a ritual that seemed to mock death. The ritual is known today as Dia de Los Muertos or Day of the Dead and is celebrated throughout Mexico. Today people don wooden skull masks called "cacaos" and dance in honor of their deceased relatives. The wooden skulls are also placed on altars that are dedicated to the dead. A relative or a friend may munch on sugar skulls, made with the names of the dead person on the forehead. Check out the excellent carvings and figurines depicting this holiday that can be found in many shops.

Día de la Revolución - Revolution Day (November 20): Celebrated throughout Mexico, 20 November marks the day in 1910 when the war to overthrow the dictator General Porfirio Diaz began. The revolution was fought due to the growing disparity between the rich landowners and the rest of the population who were mainly poor peasants and farmers. Colorful parades, speeches, and parties mark the day.

DECEMBER

Festival de Guadalupe—The Virgin of Guadalupe (December 12): December 12 is arguably the most important day of the year for millions of Catholics across Mexico as they honor a figure that is considered to be the centerpiece of the Catholic faith in their country.

Las Posadas—Christmas (December 16-24): Posadas are a Mexican Christmas tradition that takes place from December 16 to 24th. Every night in throughout Cozumel, processions take place leading to a chosen home. They carry candles and often an image of the Virgin Mary. When they reach the door of the home they sing a special Posada song in which those outside sing the part of Joseph asks for shelter and the family inside responds singing the part of the innkeeper saying that there is no room. The song switches back and forth a few times until finally the innkeeper decides to let them in. The door is opened and everyone goes inside. Inside the house there is a celebration, which can vary from a very big fancy party to a small get-together among friends. The host gives the guests food and drinks and there are piñatas with candy for the children .

La Rama (December 16): As with most customs in Mexico, La Rama came from Indian rituals and in this case is an extension of an Aztec ceremony commemorating the rebirth of nature. Officially starting December 16, it generally involves self-organized groups of children who decorate a branch from a tree or plant and then go from door to door shouting "cantamos la rama?" (Can we sing the branch?). Carrying homemade lanterns and accompanied by a rhythm section of kitchen utensils, the groups launch song, always including some verses that ask the audience to give them their aguinaldo (a sort of Christmas bonus) if they are pleased with the performance.

This continues until just before Christmas Eve, when the children give their earnings to one of the children's mothers, which they will use to buy piñatas and treats for their own Christmas party.

Navidad/Nochebuena-Christmas/Christmas Eve (December 25/24): Christmas Eve is called Nochebuena in Spanish. This is the night of the last posada. Many people attend midnight mass and then have a dinner together with their families. Christmas Day is generally a quiet day. Gifts are not traditionally exchanged on Christmas, but this is changing, and Santa Claus is becoming increasingly more prominent in Mexican Christmas celebrations.
During the holiday season there will be a giant Christmas tree in the square or the park at the palacio and other decorations. An assortment of holiday entertainment will also be going on, all for free

Vacation in Paradise!!!

Pool at Paradise Beach.

CHAPTER I

GENERAL INFORMATION

The basics you need to know.

GENERAL INFORMATION

ENTRY REQUIREMENTS: A valid passport is now required for all U.S. Citizens traveling abroad. No longer can you use a birth certificate and photo I.D.

U.S. Consulate: Ann R. Harris, Consular Agent Plaza Villa Mar en El Centro, Plaza Principal, (Parque Juarez between Melgar and 5th Ave.) 2nd floor, Locales #8 and 9, telephone (52) (987) 872-4574.

Emergency—Dial 060 If you need to talk to someone who speaks English, say "Necesito hablar con alguin que comprende ingles."

Non-Emergency Police: Main station is at Melgar between Gonzalo Guerrero & Calle 13; 872-0409

Language: English is widely spoken in Cozumel, but Spanish is the official language. A small percent still speak some Mayan on the island. If you at least attempt a little bit of Spanish it is appreciated and you will be helped along.

Water Temperature: The water temperature averages 77 degrees Fahrenheit in the winter and 85 in summer. Although these temperatures sound warm and cozy, a light to medium wetsuit or skin may be needed.

Time Zone: Cozumel is in the Central time zone. Day light savings time does not always follow the same schedule as the rest of North America.

Documents: Passport and temporary tourist card. (FMT)

WEATHER: Cozumel has two primary seasons, rainy season, which is mid-May to mid-October, and dry season the rest of the year.

Do not let rainy season keep you away, as they seldom have a rainy day as we know it. Usually a short shower or two and the sun is right back out. Temperatures are warm here all year long ranging from the nineties to the low seventies, seldom dropping below seventy on a cool winter evening. Humidity is similar to what is experienced in Florida with higher humidly in the summer months.

CLOTHING: Please ladies; remember that bathing suits belong at the beach and pool and not on public streets. Gentlemen keep a shirt on when walking around town. Cozumel is a very family oriented community and the locals frown on extensive displays of bare flesh anywhere other than at the beach.

Light cotton clothing is best suited to the climate here. You will need little more than shorts, tee- shirts and bathing suits. A nice pair of slacks and a collared shirt for the men, and a skirt or dress pants for the ladies should be packed. You will want these if you plan to dine at one of the fancier restaurants, to attend church, or if you are invited by a local to attend some special event. Bring a light jacket or sweater for a cool evening and a sweatshirt for after diving. Add a pair of sandles and a pair of sneakers and you will have everything you need.

MEDICAL: Cozumel has excellent clinics and hospitals, good doctors who speak English, dentists, and even three chiropractors. Please refer to Chapter 10 for names and phone numbers of medical providers.

TIPPING: When tipping or not, please remember that the minimum wage in Mexico is around five or six dollars a day. The workers in the Cozumel service industry depend on tips to support their families.

Waiters/waitresses: Ten to twenty percent of your check depending on quality of service. If gratuity is already included, consider leaving an additional small tip, such as the remaining pesos from your change.

Maids: two to three dollars a day left on your pillow each morning, ensures that the maid who is on duty gets the tip. If you are staying at a small hotel or B&B where it is always the same maid, you can tip at the end of your stay. I do not recommend this because if you tip daily your maid will appreciate it, and you will be amazed at the extra service above and beyond what is expected. Another thing that I and many frequent visitors do is to leave small gifts with the tips. Dollar store items are great, a small pack of crayons and coloring book for her children, small sample cosmetics, soap, etc. for the maid. They really welcome these gifts and you will receive outstanding service. At an all-inclusive, they may tell you that tips are included, please consider tipping anyway.

Dive and Fishing charters: The consensus seems to be $5 per tank tipped daily. If service is special and you had a great time because of your crew, then an extra bonus at the end of your trip will be well deserved. Remember that the tips are usually shared among the crew.

Taxi Drivers: It is not necessary to tip these drivers, but as inexpensive as the cab fares are, what's another dollar. Again you will get a big smile and a Gracias from the driver.

BANKING AND SHOPPING:
Bank and currency exchanges are normally open from nine to five. ATMs are twenty-four hour access. See chapter 10 for locations. Stores usually open about eight in the morning and stay open to very late at night. Siesta time is still practiced at some of the stores further from downtown and may be closed from one to five. See chapter 6 for shopping tips and locations.

EXCHANGE RATE:
The rate has stayed between 10 and 12 pesos to the U.S. dollar for several years, but has gone as high as 15 to 1. At this time it is hovering between 11.00 and 12.

POST OFFICE:
Located on Ave Rafael Melgar and Calle 7, it is open Monday to Friday 9-6, and on Saturday 9-12. You can mail your post cards here, but do it the first few days, as you will more than likely beat it home. You also can send telegrams here.

SHIPPING:
Pak-mail 10th Ave # 99, packs and ships. If you need something mailed to you while in Cozumel, Fed Ex, UPS, and DHL all have express service to Cozumel.

CELL PHONE USE:
In order to use your cellular phone on the Cozumel, Cancun and throughout Quintana Roo, and the Yucatan you may first have to contact your cell phone company and tell them you are going to Mexico and that you will require International Calling. Some will work without notifying them, but rates may be higher. For about $30 you can purchase a Mexican cell phone from Tel-cell or Movie Star, which comes with some credit.

CHURCH:
There are at least three Catholic Churches, a Christian Non-Denominational, a 7th Day Adventist, and several other churches on the island. See Chapter 10 Special services for more information.

PHONES:
You have several options for calling home from Mexico. There are many calling stations, which usually have the best rates. You can use your own cell phone, check with your carrier, they often have plans you can add for a few dollars to enable you to call and receive calls in Mexico. You can buy calling cards. Do not call home collect or make calls from your hotel; the charges will put you into shock.

LAUNDRY: There are Laundromats all over Cozumel. You can do it yourself or use drop off service. They will wash, dry, and fold in about two hours. I do not know what they use, but it smells so good. We used to drop off the day before we leave, and go home with all clean clothes.

GAS STATIONS: There are now four stations on the Island, Juarez and 30th Ave, Juarez and 75th Ave. on the corner of 11th and 135th, and one across from Puerto Maya. Be sure to get out of your car immediately and watch them reset the pump, some station attendants have been known to charge extra, by not resetting the pump. A small tip to the attendant is appropriate.

CHILDCARE: Most hotels offer babysitters with advance notice. If you are staying in a Villa, the management will arrange Spanish or English speaking caregivers for $5–7. There are also a couple chat boards that you can use to seek a local sitter. My daughter uses a local daycare center every time she visits with my grandson. He loves it there and it costs her about $180 pesos per day.

COZUMEL RADIO
www.cozumelradioonline.com

Wish you were in Cozumel with sand between your toes? Tune in, kick back and relax with a cool tropical blend of classic rock and island music.

If you think you have been cheated by a merchant of any type: Contact **PROFECO** (MX federal bureau of consumer protection) At the big white Municipal building on Melgar. http://www.profeco.gob.mx/

CHAPTER II

GETTING THERE

Check out your options for travel.

GETTING THERE

There are only two ways in which to arrive in Cozumel, by air or water. Most visitors that arrive by water are passengers on one of the many cruise ships that arrive daily at one of three cruise piers. These tourists get to sample Cozumel for a few short hours, but it is this small taste that often brings them back by plane for a longer stay.

The others that arrive by water are passengers on either the people ferries, or the car ferry, or the occasional private yacht like Mr. Bill Gates. It is possible to drive your own vehicle to Cozumel for an extended visit, but you will have to bring it across on the car ferry out of Calica, near Playa del Carmen. The cost for the car ferry is approximately $50.00.

The passengers on the two people ferries from Playa del Carmen have usually flown into Cancun and either taken the bus or a van to Playa del Carmen. This is a popular option as there are many better airfare deals into Cancun, than there are into Cozumel. Of course you can fly directly into the Cozumel airport via several commercial carriers and several charter carriers.

Taxicabs are only allowed to drop off at the airport, but not allowed to pick up. You will have to take a Collectivo van at a cost of $5.00– $20.00 and will make many stops. If you would like to save and take a taxi, just walk out of the airport and across the street where you can easily flag one down.

AIRLINES SERVING COZUMEL AND CANCUN

Aero México
www.aeromexico.com   1-800-237-6639

Air Canada
www.aircanada.com   1-888-247-2262

Air Tran
www.airtran.com   1-800-247-8726

American Airlines
www.aa.com   1-800-433-7300

Continental Airlines
www.continental.com   1-800-523-3273

Delta Airlines
www.delta.com   1-800-221-1212

Frontier Airlines
www.frontierairlines.com   1-800-432-1FLY (359)

Mayair
www.mayair.com.mx/   011(52) 998 8819400

Mexicana Air
www.mexicana.com   1-800531-7921

Northwest Air
www.nwa.com   1-800-225-2525

Spirit Airlines
www.spiritair.com   1-800-772-7117

Sun Country Air
www.suncountry.com   1-800-359-6786

U S Airways
www.usairways.com   1-800-622-1015

United Airlines
www.united.com   1-800-864-8331

CHARTERS

Adventure Tours
www.atusa.com   1-800-642-8872.

Funjet Vacations
www.funjet.com   1-866-558-6654

Worry-free Vacations
www.worryfreevacations.com   1-888-225-5658

DISCOUNT AIRFARES

Sky Auction
www.skyauction.com

You can often get a very good deal at this site. I have used them without any problem.

Fly Cheap Abroad
www.flycheapabroad.com

I have found my best fares at this site. You may have to play with your dates.

Latin Discount Air
www.latindiscountair.com

They have some very good fares.

Kayak
www.kayak.com

CANCUN AIRPORT BUS SCHEDULE-RIVIERA BUS/FERRY TO COZUMEL

If you find a great fare into Cancun, by all means grab it. The transportation to Playa del Carmen by bus and then to Cozumel by ferry is easy and reasonable. Buses are comfortable and air-conditioned. Trip takes approximately 45 minutes to Playa.

BUS SCHEDULE Fare is $116 pesos or $10.00

Cancun Airport to Playa Del Carmen: 1000 AM, 1040 AM, 1120 AM, 1200 PM, 1240 PM, 130 PM, 200 PM, 240 PM, 330 PM, 430 PM, 510 PM, 550 PM, 615 PM, 715 PM, 830 PM, 930 PM

Playa del Carmen to Cancun Airport: 505 AM, 750 AM, 830 AM, 920 AM, 1000 AM, 1040 AM, 1120 AM, 1200 PM, 1240 PM, 120 PM, 210 PM, 310 PM, 410 PM, 500 PM, 550 PM, 715 PM

Bus system: http://www.ado.com.mx

You may buy your ticket from the driver or agent at the bus, or at one of the windows just before you leave the building.

FERRY SCHEDULE Fare is approximately $12.00 or 160 pesos each way.

Only purchase one way ticket or you may have to wait extra hours for the right ferry company. Trips are added and deleted during different seasons, so be sure to verify your schedule the day before.

Ultramar
987-869-3223 <u>www.ultramar.com.mx</u>

Mexico Waterjet
987-872-1578 / 1508 **www.mexicowaterjets.com**

Playa del Carmen to Cozumel: 6:00am then every hour on the hour 8:00am–12:00pm and 2:00pm, 4:00pm, 5:00pm, 6:00pm, 8:00pm, 10:00pm

Cozumel to Playa del Carmen: 5:00am then every hour on the hour 7:00am–11:00am and 1:00pm, 3:00pm, 4:00pm, 5: 10:00pm, 7:00pm, 9:00pm

Ferry schedule may change, as everything in Mexico is prone to do. You need to confirm schedule when planning travel. There are two ferry companies and the last I knew they were rotating every hour rather than run at the same time.

Vehicle Ferry

Calica to Cozumel

Tuesday-Saturday 4:00am, 8:00am, 1:00pm, 6:00pm
Sunday 6:00am, 6:00pm Monday 8:00am, 6:00 pm

Cozumel to Calica:

Tuesday and Saturday 6:00am, 11:00am, 4:00pm, 8:00pm
Sunday 8:00am, 8:00pm Monday 11:00am, 8:00pm

The price each way for a car and driver is 555 pesos (approx. $47), each extra passenger in the car must pay 60 pesos (approx. $5). A promotional rate is sometimes available. Larger vehicles must pay more - contact. Transcaribe for prices.

For more information contact Trans Del Caribe in Cozumel at 987-872-7688 or visit their website **www.transcaribe.com.mx**

TIP: *At the bus station and ferry terminals you will see men on large tricycles. They are called tricyclos and will take your entire luggage to the ferry, or from the ferry. No set cost, just tip him well.*

The tricyclo man who helps with your luggage.

CHAPTER III

WHERE TO STAY

You have many choices for lodging in Cozumel.

Lodging options in Cozumel range from small family run hotels and B&Bs to all-inclusive mega resorts where you never have to leave the property during vacation. It would be a shame to choose the latter and never get a chance to experience the true flavor of Cozumel. We recommend that even if you stay at an all-inclusive property, that you still venture into town to shop, eat dinner at a local restaurant, and mingle with the people. I promise you will not be disappointed.

Another wonderful option is to rent a casa or villa. Become part of the neighborhood; meet the neighbors, shop at the Mercado and experiment with Mexican food and recipes in your own kitchen. Relax at your own private pool without a crowd, even go skinny-dipping if you would like.

When you rent a villa or casa, it is often less than the cost of a hotel room if the cost is shared with others. Maid service is included and you can even hire a cook for your stay. Whichever you choose, relax and enjoy your Cozumel vacation.

Rates may be higher or lower than listed. You should contact the facility or check their web sites for specials and package deals.

BED & BREAKFASTS and HOSTELS

ALICIA'S B & B
www.aliciasbedandbreakfast.comt
65Ave y 65 bis y calle 19
832-615-9254
Local 987-872-5478

This bargain is located in a residential neighborhood, close to local stores and restaurants. This is just a brisk 15-minute walk to downtown or a $2–3 cab ride.

Operated by Alicia, an American expatriate and her Mayan partner Chuco, they will have you believing you are just part of the family. Chuco is also the cook here and his breakfasts are awesome, they alone are worth the price charged for a night. His guacamole is the best on the island.

There is no pool here, but who needs it with all the wonderful beaches and beach clubs that are available in paradise. All rooms have refrigerators, ceiling fans, and AC. There is a coffee maker, BBQ grill and area for light cooking. For divers there is a large rinse tank for your gear. Talk shop with Chuco as he used to be a dive boat captain, and loves to practice his English. I have stayed with Alicia many times and whole-heartedly can recommend this B & B.

Large rooms $35.00 per night for 2. $5 additional person Tax is included.

AMARANTO
www.tamarindoamaranto.com
Calle 5 between Ave 15 & 20
011-52-872-3219

I love this place. The bungalows are round Mayan style huts with palapa roofs. The suites in the 2 story round building are large and comfortable. Book the second floor room if you have kids, they will love the eagle's nest lookout in the palapa roof. This was my boy's favorite place. Jorge is a warm and friendly host. He will help you with lots of information.
Rates $49-69

AMIGO'S SUPERHOSTEL COZUMEL
www.bacalar.net
Calle 7 #571 between Aves 25 and 30
011-52-987-872-3868

This former B&B is now a upscale hostel with two 8 bed bunk rooms and one 3 bed room. It is within easy walking distance to shopping and downtown interests and restaurants. Nice swimming pool area, bikes available for guests. Rates starting at $12 per person.

B & B CARIBO
www.cozumel.net/bb/caribo
Corner of Juarez and Ave 40
011-52-987-872-3195

Formerly known as a Bed and Breakfast, they are now an Extended Stay Hotel with rooms and apartments priced from $200 to $300 (USD) per WEEK. Each room has a refrigerator, Apartments have full Kitchen, and all units have private bathroom, shower and hot water.

There is a roof top garden with beautiful view. Close to downtown restaurants, local movie theater and shopping. No pool, but easy access to beaches.

BALDWINS GUEST HOUSE
www.moosepages.com
Ave 55 between Calle 1 and Salas Ave
011-52-987-872-1148

Dale and Kathy, a very warm and friendly couple, own this wonderful little B&B. Set behind an 8 ft. privacy wall you will find a small piece of paradise among the beautiful flowers and fruit trees. Beautifully decorated rooms, a casita, and a 3-bedroom house are available for your stay. A large pool area, outdoor kitchen and an entertainment gazebo provide for all your needs. Relax in a hammock with a good book, or for a peaceful siesta. A full breakfast is served each morning.
Rates range from $75.00–150.00 double

BEACH HOUSE HOSTEL
beachousecozumel@gmail.com
Cozumel Country Club
011-52-987- 87 2 62 85

This is an upscale hostel situated in the Cozumel Country Club, a nice quite neighborhood, 5 Km. north of San Miguel Downtown. They are getting great reviews all around. Breakfast is not included but they do serve coffee and pastries in the morning. There is a great pool to enjoy, free internet, and friendly owners. Children are welcome.
Rates: $25-$69

CORAL REEF INN
www.cozumelcoralreefinn.com
Ave5 between Calle17&19
011-52-987-872-7390
888-843-5717

The rooms are cozy and have pillow top king or queen size beds, quality linens, quiet high-efficiency mini-split air-conditioners with remote controls, cable televisions, mini-fridges & high-speed Wi-Fi internet. Each room has a large bathroom with two-person showers. Breakfast is not provided, but there is a full kitchen available for your use.
Rates $55-$85 Good discounts on weekly and dive packages.

HOSTELITO
hostelitocozumelmx@ gmail.com
Ave 10 between Benito Juarez and Calle 2
052- 987- 86-9 815711

This is an affordable and clean hostel; it's only a short walk to San Miguel Historical Church and the Main Plaza where most of the restaurants, bars, banks, and all kind of services are located. It is ideal for the budget conscious traveler or back-packer, who is looking for comfortable, clean, spacious, and well located lodging. It has a 26 bed mixed dorm, a 4-6 bed private room, and a private double. Internet access is available for free.
Rates: $12 Dorm, $10 PP in 6 man room, $17.50 PP in Double

LAS LUNAS INN BED AND BREAKFAST
www.laslunas.com
Ave 40 # 265 between Calle 6 & 4
011-52-987-872-0111
303-459-2228

A small B&B catering to scuba diver, the owners are Oliver and Jamie Robertson, a couple with a passion for diving. Rooms are basic, but roomy and comfortable The .B&B consists of 3 rooms, with shared bath, and a casita with private bath and refrigerator. No pool, but who cares, if you will be diving every day. A continental breakfast of fresh fruit, pastries, and cereals is included.
$55.00-$75.00 double Casita
$69.00 double

MI CASA EN COZUMEL
www.micasaencozumel.com
Ave5 #543 between 7th & 9th
011-562- 987-872 6200

This small hotel, modern but very cool, sits right in the heart of downtown Cozumel. Just one block away from the main street and waterfront with its wonderful views, also one block from the largest shopping area in town, just 4 blocks away from the main plaza and the ferry pier to the mainland, and walking distance to most restaurants and bars. There is a Jacuzzi but no pool. Breakfast is included. There are rooms and suites available.
Rates $40 - $175

SUMMER PLACE INN
www.cozumelinn.com
Ave 10 #1119 between Calle 17 & 19
011-52-987-872-6300

A large beautiful B&B. Rooms are large and spacious and beautifully decorated. There is a large pool for swimming or just floating and relaxing. Breakfast is self-serve and there is a fully stocked refrigerator available 24 hours a day. Enjoy the beautiful gardens and hammocks for siesta. Equipment storage and rinse tank, bikes, and wave boards are available. It is located two blocks from the ocean, with easy access to shopping and dining. Laundry is available on site. Wireless internet provided.

This B&B can be rented by the room, or the entire complex. Total occupancy is 18.

April 1–Dec 15 $65.00 double $450.00 week $3000 entire complex
Dec 15–April 1 $95.00 double $630.00 week $4000 entire complex

TAMARINDO'S BED AND BREAKFAST
www.tamarindocozumel.com
Calle 4 between Ave 20 y 25
011-52-987-872-3614

Hosted by Eliane who will be happy to assist you anyway she can. A small nicely decorated B&B with 5 rooms, each having private bath and cable TV and ceiling fans. Only 2 rooms have AC, but the ceiling fans cool nicely.

Breakfast is prepared and served by Eliane with a clearly French influence, as Eliane is from Normandy, France. Her breakfasts are enough to hold you well until lunch. Wireless internet connection is available, so bring your laptop. It is an easy walk to downtowns shopping and dining. No pool. There are 2 new suites with kitchenettes that do not include breakfast.
Rates $48 - $72

VILLA ANNA MARIA
info@mayaroute.org
Ave 65bis No 171, at Rosado Salas

Villa Anna Maria is located just 10 minutes from the tourist area. This is a beautiful villa with 8 Mediterranean style rooms each with private bathroom. It is a beautiful place, nice full garden, very friendly owner and staff who treat you like family.
Rates start @ $35 single

VILLA ESCONDIDA
www.villaescondidacozumel.com
10th Ave #299, between Calle3 & Salas
011 52 987 869 2203

This is a brand new B & B located in the heart of Cozumel. They have 4 beautiful guestrooms to choose from. There is a nice pool, palapa, honor bar, satellite TV, games, and DVDs. Free beer if anyone can beat David at checkers! Another nice benefit is day use of beach condo (when available), at "Playa San Juan". Bikes are available free for your pleasure. It is currently rated #1 B&B on Trip Advisor. This is an adult's only lodging. Rates: $75 - $99 Tax included

ECONOMY HOTELS

HOTEL AGUILAR
www.cozumel-hotels.net/aguilar
haguilar@coznet.finred.com.mx
Ave 3 #98 between Melgar & Ave5
011-52-987-872-0307

This is a small basic hotel popular with divers and those on a budget. They are located just one block from the pier and three blocks from the Plaza. It is an easy stroll to shopping, dining, and dive boat pick-ups.

All rooms have AC, ceiling fans refrigerator, and TVs are available for a fee. Rooms are very basic with two double beds, nightstand, and dresser. Most important is that they are kept very clean. Nice pool area for after diving relaxation.
Rates start at $45 but check for specials.

BAHIA SUITES
www.suitesbahia.com
Melgar Ave & Calle 3
Downtown 27 rooms

If you are here purely for the diving and do not need a lot of extras, this is the place. Just 20 steps from the downtown piers, makes it very convenient for dive boat pickups. Rooms are large, bright and comfortable, furnished with either a king size bed or a king and a double. Rooms include AC, ceiling fans, satellite TV, and kitchenettes. Request one of the ocean front rooms that are on each floor, some have balconies. Right in the center of Cozumel's best shopping and dining. A continental breakfast of coffee, pastries and fresh fruit is included.
Rates: $59 – 95 plus tax

HOTEL BARRACUDA

www.cozumel-hotels.net/barracuda
barracudahotelczm@prodigy.net.mx
628 Rafael Melgar Ave
866-327-1389
011-52-987-872-0002

Everything a diver could want at an economical price. Good shore diving from the hotel beach, private pier for pick up, Dive Paradise dive shop on site and even lockers for your gear, but be sure to bring your own lock. Rooms are simply furnished but large and roomy, with AC, ceiling fans, and refrigerator. TV is $2 additional. The rooms above the first floor have small balconies with awesome Caribbean views. Dining, shopping, and nightclubs are a short walk from the hotel. Shop for your essentials, drinks and snacks from Chedraui or enjoy a show at the cinema, both a 2 minute stroll across the street. There is the No-Name Bar at poolside, with some pretty good food. Also on site are a Calling & computer center, book exchange, and a health salon even staffed with chiropractors.
Rates: $68- $120 includes tax

HOTEL BELLO CARIBE

www.bellocaribe.com.mx
bcaribe@prodigy.net.mx
#660 Pedro Joaquin Coldwell Ave (30th Ave)
011-52-987-872-6520

Small family hotel located only 3 minutes from the airport, making it great for those early morning flights. The rooms are good sized and decorated in pretty pastels and bamboo. There is a large pool area and tropical gardens for your enjoyment. There is a small restaurant on site. There is also a very large palapa room for parties and large gatherings. Lodging is available for singles to 4 bedroom suites.
Rates: $400 MP to $1,480 MP

CASA VIENTO

www.casaviento.net
Country Club Estates
011-52- 987-869-8220
Across from the golf course

This is a small boutique hotel with excellent room offerings. I have placed it in the budget category because all rooms have either a full kitchen or kitchenette, which enables you to cook your own meals. Every review of this little gem praises the owners Nicole and Raul. They say it is like staying with good friends or family.

They offer 4 studio rooms and 2 apartment suites, one of which has 2 bedrooms. Relax by the pool with a good book or morning coffee from the free coffee bar. Rates $75-165

CASITA de MAYA
www.casitademaya.com
info@casitademaya.com
Ave 65 & Aero Puerto
011-52- 987-869-2606

Gives a new meaning to "Airport hotel", this awesome little hotel is literally steps away from the airport. The only thing lacking here are additional rooms, but then that is part of what makes it special. All four rooms are poolside, brand new and tastefully furnished. Amenities include a small refrigerator, hair dryer, microwave, alarm clock, and internet connection for your laptop. There is even a small "dive bar" where you can relax with a cold cerveza while watching big screen TV. Island Dan is the American owner, who will go out of his way to help you with rental cars, tours, directions; he will even meet you at the airport with a cold cerveza. What more could you ask for? Worth the rack rates and more! Dan's place is currently #1 on Trip Advisor!
Rates: $59–$109 but check for specials.

HOTEL COLONIAL
www.suitescolonial.com
Ave 5 & Calle 3
reservaciones@suitescolonial.com
Downtown on Plaza
877-228-6747
28 rooms and suites
011-52-987-872-9090

One of the hottest spots in town for people watching. This may be a small hotel, but it offers nice rooms and amenities. The balcony looks straight down into the plaza, which gives you a front row seat for the Sunday evening activities and a good view of Carnaval happenings. Be sure to book way ahead if you want a room during Carnaval. Rooms and suites are simply decorated, but large and well equipped with AC, refrigerator, and TV. Suites have living room and kitchenette. Decent pool area is available to relax in. Includes a continental breakfast served each morning in the lobby. Internet access is also available in lobby. Rates: $59.00–$89.00

HOTEL COSTA BRAVA

www.cozumel-hotels.net/costa_brava
cosbrava@prodigy.net.mx
601 Rafael Melgar
In Town
011-52-987-872-1290

Welcome to the Hacienda! This will be your first thought as you arrive at the hotel. A small hotel built in traditional hacienda style architecture, with a beautiful garden and palapa area. A BBQ is set up in the garden so that you can grill what you catch. This is a small, basic hotel, but very clean rooms with AC and cable TV in each room. Mega value for your dollar.
Rates: $45.00–$55.00

HOTEL DULCE

contacto@dulcehotel.com
www.hostelplanet.com/hostelplanet.com
Adolfo Rosado Salas #72
011-52-987-869-1604
Cell 987-118-6413

This is a small hotel located in the heart of the action. It is located half a street away from the oceanfront. They are a short walk to the ferry, next to shops, diving areas, restaurants and bars. They offer free Wi-Fi in rooms and lobby, Air Conditioning, TV in rooms, 24 hour tourist information and continental breakfast.
Rates : $36-$40

HOTEL EL MARQUES

www.cozumel-hotels.net/el_marques
180 Ave 5
011-52-987-872-0677
In Town 40 rooms

This place is located right on the Plaza.. Small clean local hotel with fair sized rooms that are simply decorated. All have AC, which will mute the noise from the Plaza and street. Run by a friendly smiling staff and night watchman. This is a terrific location for access to dining and shopping.
No pool area.
Rates: $35 - $55

EL PIRETA
Ave 5 between Calle 1 & Salas
011- 52-987- 872-0051
Just off the Plaza
Small local hotel—not reviewed. The lobby looked old but clean when I stopped
for a visit.
$33.00 double w/fan $40.00 double w/AC

HOTEL FLORES
011-52-987-872-0051
Salas between Melgar & Ave 5

In the heart of San Miguel Town, just a couple steps from the main Avenue and only
half block from the oceanfront and main pier is Hotel Flores, a small and traditional
hotel since 1970. Recently remodeled offers you 18 standard rooms, 4 triplets and
4 single rooms. Rooms are kept clean with daily maid service. Wi-Fi is available in
the lobby. Some rooms with AC and some only have fans.
Rates: Start @ $200 MP

HOTEL ISLA ESMERALDA
www.hotelislaesmeralda.com
Call2betweenAve20&25
011-52-987-872-3255

This is a small locally owned hotel. It is furnished plainly with handmade furniture
in average sized rooms. It has a small courtyard with a pool to cool off in. There
is now a small coffee shop on the premises. It is located in the middle of town and
an easy walk to shopping and dining. Mostly Spanish speaking unless the owner is
there. A good value for the Peso!
Rates: $30 - $53

HOTEL KAREY
011-52-987-872-2011
Ave 25 & Salas

This is a small local hotel with very basic but clean rooms. Rooms have ceiling fans
but AC is extra. It has a small pool and courtyard.
$275 MP (app $27) Fan $300 MP (app $30) AC

HOTEL LA CASONA REAL

hccasonareal@hotmail.com
www.hotel-la-casona-real-cozumel.com
501 Juarez Ave and 25th Ave

011-52-987-872-5471

This is small local hotel with small simple rooms that have recently been redone..
All rooms have AC. Nice pool area with lounge chairs and dining available poolside.
It sometimes gets noisy from the streets, but if AC is running you will not hear it. It
is just a short 5-block walk to the Plaza. They have recently added a restaurant for
breakfast and lunch.
Rates: $50.00–$55.00 the suite is $80; 10% discount for weekly stays.

HOTEL MARY CARMEN

4 Ave 5
info@hotelmarycarmen.com
011-52-987-872-0581
866-613-9330
In Town 30 rooms

Small Mexican hotel owned and operated by a nice family. The hotel is built right on
the pedestrian walkway in the center of town. The two floors of rooms rise around a
sunken, open patio inside the building. The rooms are basic and clean with cold AC.
It is right in the middle of shopping, dining and nightlife.
Rates: $35.00–$45.00

PALMA DORADA INN

www.cozumel-hotels.net/pdi
#44 A.R.Salas Ave between Ave 5&10
011-52-987-872-0330

Small basic family run hotel. The rooms are good sized, clean and simple, but very
colorful. Staff is very friendly. Offers free pastries and coffee in the morning. Close
to dining and shopping.
Rates $38 - $72

HOTEL PEPITA

www.hotelpepitacozumel.com
Ave 15 #120
011-52-987-872-0098
In Town

Good choice for people on a budget, or wanting to spend their dollars on more important things. It is popular with visitors from many other countries. This little place has clean basic rooms with showers, AC, cable TV, no phone. Five minute walk to the main plaza for shopping and dining. Enjoy a round of mini golf and sangria at Cozumel Mini golf right down the street. No pool
Rates start @ $39

PLAZA COZUMEL
www.hotelplazacozumel.com
#3 Calle 2 (½ block to waterfront)
011-52-987-872-2700
In Town 61 rooms

This has got to be one of the best-kept secrets on Cozumel. This budget hotel has roof top pool and bar with an amazing Caribbean ocean view, not what you would expect at their prices. Small but clean and brightly decorated rooms with AC and cable TV. It is just steps away from the museum which you should not miss, and close to the Plaza, shopping, dining, and piers. Register on their web site and get discounted rates.
Rates: $50 +

POSADA EDEM
www.posadaedem.com/english.html
Calle 2 between Ave 5 & 10
011-52-987-872

Small family hotel, with small functional rooms decorated in pink. Some rooms have AC. Close to Plaza and downtown areas for dining and shopping, Friendly staff.
$22.00 double/fan $28.00 double/AC

POSADA LETTY
011-52-987-872-0257
Calle 1 & Ave 15
In Town

This is a small local hotel with basic rooms, ceiling fans, no AC. Wi-Fi is now available free of charge. First floor rooms are light and airy. It is just a short walk to the Plaza, dining, and shopping. Run by a very warm and friendly family.
$200 MP

SAFARI INN

www.aquasafari.com/safariinn.html
Melgar #429 between Calles 5&7
011-52-987-872-0101
Downtown
SKYPE AQUA.DONNA

The Safari Inn is a small 12 room hotel located waterfront above the Aqua Safari Dive Shop. The rooms are simple yet clean, modern, and comfortable. The rooms are large and can accommodate more than 2 persons. At these prices you will have more money to spend on diving. Rates $40 double $5 extra per person up to 5 people. They also have great dive packages.

VILLAGE TAN KAH

www.villagetankah.com
Close to Park Royal
Costera Sur KM 3.5
011-52-987- 872-6142

This has got to be one of the best-kept secrets on Cozumel. There are large suites with bed/beds seating area and kitchen area. The rooms are very comfortably furnished in traditional Mexican style. Relax at the pool or chill in a hammock. They offer some awesome dive packages with Blue Bubble Divers and Scuba Shack. Room and Suites: $64-$130

MODERATE HOTELS

BLUE ANGEL RESORT

www.blueangelresort.com
Melgar Ave south of town 1¼ miles
Waterfront
011- 52- 987- 872 -7258
866- 779 -9986

This little family run hotel gets 5 star reviews from visitors. Resort was formerly known as the Lorena or Caribe Blu for you Cozumel old timers. You get a sunset performance that is unforgettable. The shore is a rocky front, not a sandy beach, but do not let this stop you from enjoying some great snorkeling and diving only steps from your doorway. On site is Blue Angel Dive shop and a small restaurant serving breakfast and lunch. There is a nice size fresh water pool. Rooms are furnished with

2 double or 1 king bed, and have a balcony to watch the sunset from. TV, safe, AC, and phone are standard. It is a brisk walk or short cab ride to town.
Rates start @ $89 double

CASA DEL MAR

www.casadelmarcozumel.com
reservations@casadelmar.com
Melgar Ave 2 ½ miles south of town
011- 52- 987- 872-1900
Ocean View 98 rooms/8 cabanas

It is like a Howard Johnson's type hotel with a few extra frills. The views of the Caribbean sunsets are the best thing about this property. Rooms are clean, basic, middle class Mexico. Reserve one of the 2 story cabanas if you can, they come with a small kitchenette. Pool area is nice, but beach area across the street is small and nearly non-existent. You do get the use of Nachi CoCom a very nice beach club further south. The breakfast here is reported to be excellent, but other meals receive mixed reviews. Good deals are to be found on the Internet that will be way below the listed rack rates.
Rack Rates $79.00–$254.00

CASA MEXICANA

www.casamexicana.com
reservaciones@casaamericanacozumel.com
#457 Melgar Ave
877-228-6747
011-52-987-872-9073
WOW! This modern Mexican architecture stands out, yet seems to belong. One of the newer buildings in Cozumel's inventory of hotels, thet building was awarded 1st place by Modern Mexican Architecture's regional biennial for Design. The furnishings are outstanding; beds, desks, and all wooden furniture are hand carved Mayan wood. Enjoy sunbathing at the pool on the second story while gazing out at the Caribbean Sea, beautiful on a starlit night. During the day you can watch the cruise ships come and go. There is also an indoor pool with poolside bar. Rooms have balconies, TV, phone, refrigerator, and even plush bathrobes. It is definitely first class for a moderate price. Breakfast buffet is included and served on the terrace.
Rates $115–195 double check Internet for great deals

EL CID LA CEIBA

www.elcid.com
cozumel@elcid.com.mx
South Zone Beachfront

Near Puerta Maya 71 rooms
800-435-3240
011-52-987-872-0844

A longtime favorite of the wet suit crowd, they continue to offer excellent dive packages. If you are looking for a wonderful place to stay, right on the water, with beautiful garden walk-troughs, spectacular restaurant on the water, and the best most personal service you could imagine, this is the place. Rooms are quite large and beautifully decorated, and come with small balconies which are handy for drying dive gear. All rooms have AC, satellite TV, and VCR, with movie rentals available at the front desk. There is a dive operation on site, pools, a small sandy beach, and a fitness center. Request a tower room, these have been recently renovated and have incredible views. Cruise ships dock almost in front. Some people enjoy it, and others complain about it. They also have day pass users from the ships.
Rates start at $85.00 double AI option is available. Check Internet for sales.

FIESTA AMERICANA DIVE RESORT
www.fiestaamericana.com
South Zone Beach across the street
800-FIESTA-1
228 rooms AI option
011-52-987-872-9600

The biggest selling point for this property is the location, near some of the best reefs for diving and snorkeling. Rooms are good sized, and some of them have good ocean views. Avoid the casitas, it is a very long walk to the beach and pool from them, and there have been complaints of excessive bugs, probably due to their proximity to the jungle. The pool area is very nice and they have some of the most beautiful tropical gardens on Cozumel. Dive House is the dive operation on site. Chankanaab Park is a short walk from the hotel.
Rates start @ $95.00 double AI option is $55.00 additional per person

GUIDOS BOUTIQUE HOTEL
www.guidosboutiquehotel.com
Melgar Ave No.2
011-52-987-872-094652 987 87
Waterfront downtown

This new addition to Cozumel has 2 master suites and 2 junior suites, with fully equipped kitchens, dining room, living room, state of the art bathrooms and oceanfront terraces in every suite, within walking distance to restaurants, boutique stores and Cozumel`s main square. The popular

Guido's Restaurant is at the same location.
Rates: $90-$170

HACIENDA SAN MIGUEL
www.haciendasanmiguel.com
info@haciendasanmiguel.com
#500 Calle 10
In Town
866-712-6387
011-52-987-872-1986

This is absolutely stunning old Mexico, both inside and out. Rooms are large and beautiful decorated with Mexican art work. Studios, Jr suites, and a town house all come with kitchen or kitchenette. Located close to the Plaza and it is close to dining and shopping. There is no swimming pool, but there is a beautiful and peaceful fountain area and garden, perfect for some quiet time, or reading a good book. A continental breakfast is served in your room each morning, and at night you just may receive a treat of homemade cookies. Staff is friendly and treats you as part of the family.
Rates: $71.00–$187.00

HOTEL COZUMEL
www.hotelcozumel.us
Melgar about 1 mile from Plaza
877-454-4355
011-52-987-872-2855
AI Option 180 rooms
Home to Cozumel's largest swimming pool, this pool is huge with what seems like miles of lounge chairs surrounding it. There is also a second smaller pool and Jacuzzi. Rooms are nice enough, comparable to a Holiday Inn, but with plenty of space and nice large balconies. Be sure to request an ocean front room.
Snorkeling and diving from the rocky beach is lots of fun, as you will see a large assortment of marine life. Dive Paradise is the on-site dive operator, with boats leaving from the private pier. The hotel has recently added an all-inclusive option and the food reviews have run from adequate to amazing. Breakfast here is getting the highest marks. You can take the AI plan, eat breakfast and lunch there, but eat out at night, and this should still give you a good deal.
Rates start at $100 double and $75 PP if AI Again…check the Internet for bargains

HOTEL FLAMINGO
www.hotelflamingo.com
info@hotelflamiggo.com

Calle 6 between Melgar & Ave 5
800-806-1601
011-52-987-872-1264

The Flamingo is a unique boutique property located in the cultural center of Cozumel. It is just steps from the waterfront and the dining and shopping attractions of the town square. Rooms are large and decorated with Cuban art. For a real treat, rent the 2-bedroom penthouse with its awesome view of the Caribbean. They offer diving, fishing, and romantic getaway packages.
Rates: $65 - $200

HOTEL B (former Fontan)
www.hotelbcozumel.com
info@hotelbcozumel.com
011-52-987-872-0300
North Zone Beachfront

The New Hotel B is in the serene near north of Cozumel, far from the cruise ship crowds, yet close to town for the legendary restaurants and shopping. Also nearby is the Jack Nicklaus Signature golf course, Isle of Passion, horseback riding and many other enjoyable activities, all in the tranquil and beautiful north side of town. It is easy access for great snorkeling and shore diving and the lagoon offers easy entrance and exit from the water. This property has been completely redone. The guest rooms are elegant and relaxing with a panoramic view of the water.
Opening in July 2011.
Rates: unknown at publication

SABOR RESORT AND SPA
www.saboresorts.com
South Zone Beachfront
888-773-4349
011-52-987-8729300
ALL INCLUSIVE ADULTS ONLY

Formerly the Wyndham this is now an adult's only hotel. Set on a nice beach, this property consists of three story Caribbean style bungalows, which house spacious suites and studios. Single story bungalows contain the standard hotel rooms, which are plenty spacious. All are decorated in pretty soft pastels. All rooms have balconies or terraces to sit on and enjoy the ocean breezes, and the sweet smell of the jungle. Review range from fantastic to not so good. Most complaints center on the dining.
Rates can be found starting at $135

SCUBA CLUB COZUMEL

www.scubaclubcozumel.com
MelgarAve1milesouthofdowntown
011-52-987-872-0853
800-847-5708

This place is a long-time favorite of divers. The rooms are large and simple but pleasantly decorated. All rooms have AC, but TVs are viewed as an interruption of relaxation and diving…so no TV. The food served is the basic AI, with an excellent breakfast. Eat your breakfast here, walk to town for dinner, and you will still get a decent deal. Offers excellent dive packages, with dive operator on site.

Rates vary by package and diver/non diver from $296.00 for a 3 night non diving stay based on triple in Sept to $1396.00 for 7 nights/5days diving based on single. Prices are per person

VENTANAS AL MAR

www.ventanasalmar.biz/info.htm
ventanasalmar@cozumel-hotels.net
east side next to Coconuts

A unique Caribbean experience, this oceanfront hotel is located on the east side of Cozumel Island where there is always a breeze and where there are no other hotels. Wind turbines, with storage batteries, use the steady ocean breezes to produce the hotel's electricity. Beautiful cozy rooms, decorated with Mexican Rustic and Talavera accents await you.

Each room has a kitchenette with coffee maker and microwave. It is a different experience from the regular hotel stay. Breakfast is included. You really need a rental car if you stay here.

Rates $94–$184

VILLA ALDORA

www.aldoravilla.com
Oceanfront North of Town
210-569-1203
Exclusive for Aldora divers

The Villa Aldora is a unique choice in Cozumel accommodations. Consisting of 12 bedrooms and suites, proximity and interconnection can allow for that special large group/family, or just the couple desiring tranquility and Mexican charm on the beautiful near north coast of Cozumel. All rooms and suites have a private entrance; private bath and 5 have full kitchens. Those without full kitchens do have; a refrigerator, microwave, coffee maker, and utensils for light meals. Each room has cable TV, DSL broadband internet (wireless and Ethernet), and free Unlimited use of internet telephones.

Villa Aldora is located just north of town, on the main beachfront road of Cozumel just south of the marina, Puerto Abrigo. From there it is a simple walk into the main part of town. Enjoy the stunning views of the turquoise Caribbean from almost all rooms.
Rates $85-295

VILLA BLANCA GARDEN BEACH HOTEL
www.villablanca.net
Melgar about 2 miles South of Plaza
011-52-987-872-0730

This is a beachfront hotel located approximately 5 miles from Cozumel Airport and two miles from town, right in front of **Villa Blanca Reef and Wall**. It's a great place for snorkeling and shore diving. The beach is a rocky shore and you will need beach shoes. Included on the property are a swimming pool, Jacuzzi, poolside bar, tennis, gourmet and casual restaurant, snack bar, beach club with private pier for hotel guests, three dive shops, wireless Internet, gym, handicapped access, and mini-market.
Rooms available are standard, superior, villas, and pent house. All are nicely furnished and includes a kitchenette. 5
Rates: $63 - $250
VILLAS EL ENCANTO
www.villaselencantocozumel.com
Calle 21 between Melgar and Ave 5
011-52-987-869-0008

This is a beautiful property and perfect for a relaxing vacation. It is surrounded by tropical gardens and jungle, located 3 blocks from the commercial areas and 1 block from the sea. The rooms are large and bright with cold AC and confortable beds. There is a kitchen and living room available for use.
Rates $70-100

VILLA LAS ANCLAS
www.lasanclas.com
Ave5 #325 between Calle 3&5
01152 9 8787 25476

Small, quiet, intimate hotel, made up of spacious suites arranged along a shady, serene tropical garden. Each suite has two floors with living, dining and kitchenette areas on the first floor, and a queen size bedroom with bath on the second floor. No pool. Rates $95–$125

VISTA DEL MAR
www.hotelvistadelmar.com
info@hotelvistadelmar.com
Between Calle 5&7
Waterfront
888-309-9988

Rooms are decorated in a cozy elegant Mexican style using wood, shells, mosquito netting and natural materials. My daughter is in love with their original headboards. This is also a great spot to be during Carnaval. You can stand on your balcony and catch beads, or throw them to the kids. Rooms are clean and comfortable with great views. Close to everything.
No pool but has a large Jacuzzi.
Rates $78–$120

EXPENSIVE

ALLEGRO COZUMEL
www.occidentalhotels.com/allegro/Cozumel.asp
Beachfront
800-858-2558

This is a beautiful property whose buildings consist of 2 story Polynesian thatched roof villas. It is located on one of Cozumel's favorite white beaches San Francisco beach. It has children's pool and waterpark, with lots of activities for the kids. The on-site dive shop gets rave reviews. There have been a few negative reviews predominantly regarding the food. This is an all-inclusive property.
Rates: $120-$400

AURA SUITES
www.auraresorts.com
South Zone Beachfront
888-773-4349
011-52-987-8729300
ALL INCLUSIVE ADULTS ONLY

This is an all-suites hotel operated by the same company as Sabor. every one of the 87 hotel rooms is actually a suite. The smallest being a spectacular 750+ square feet and the largest suites are a sprawling 1,500 square feet. The adults-only policy means it's just that much more peaceful here. All boast an ocean view and have private furnished outdoor space; some even have a personal lap pool. Free Wi-fi, iPod docks, and flat screen HD TVs just make things a little nicer.
Rates can be found starting around $300 per couple.

CORAL PRINCESS
www.coralprincess.com
reservations@coralprincess.com
North Zone Beachfront
800-253-2702
011-598872-3200

Set on a private beach about 10 minutes north of town. The pool area grounds are beautiful with a definite Caribbean feel. The rooms range from a standard room, which I thought were a little tight for space, and one, two, and three bedroom suites. The suites are much roomier. All are decorated beautifully in eye appealing colors. There are two on site restaurants here and reviews were decent. An American breakfast in included for adults. The bars offer 2 for one drinks at happy hour.
Rates $132–$627.00

COZUMEL PALACE
www.palaceresorts.com
Melgar Ave In town
800-635-1836
011-52-987-872-9430
Waterfront

Palace Resorts scores big time with their newest 5 star resort. Previously known as Plaza Las Glorias, the building was totally renovated and opened May 2005.
If you want true pampering, 5 star accommodations, and amenities, this is THE place. Every room is ocean view with a balcony and a Jacuzzi in the room. The furnishings are elegant, quiet AC, ceiling fans, room safe, coffee maker, mini bar, bathrobes and more. There are two swimming pools, one with swim up bar and a dive operation on site. The only negative point is that there is no beach, but the pool is oceanfront. You will be pampered and treated as royalty here. The prices are steep, but good deals can be found on the Internet.
Rates start at $278 pp. all-inclusive

EL COZUMELENO RESORT

www.elcozumeleno.com
reserva@elczumeleno.com
North Zone Beachfront
ALL INCLUSIVE 252 rooms
800-437-3923
011-52-987-872-9530

This property receives high marks for its large sandy white beach. The beautiful free-form pool with waterfall is a pleasure to spend time at.

Snorkeling is good from the beachfront. Activity is never ending here, with a staff that strives to make your vacation fun; you can even play beach bingo. Food is slightly better than the usual all-inclusive fare, but some customers report difficulty obtaining tables at the reservations only restaurant.
Rooms are spacious and decorated in pretty pastels. The AC is COLD, great after a day in the humidity. Bring your own beach towels here, as they have a $50.00 fee for lost towels.
Rates $85–$195 PP all inclusive

IBEROSTAR RESORT

www.iberostar.co
South Zone Beachfront
305-774-9225
ALL INCLUSIVE 306 rooms

This resort has some of the most beautiful grounds on the island, well maintained tropical gardens with peacocks and peahens roaming freely, lots of iguanas, and colorful parrots in cages. The beach is a bit of a disappointment, as it is more rocky than sandy. Be sure to bring beach shoes to protect your feet. Rooms are of average size, furnished nicely with all the basic amenities, AC, safe, TV. The AI food is the usual for an AI, with a good breakfast, the other meals acceptable. With Palancar Reef at your doorstep it is a good place for divers, and there is an on-site dive operation.
Rates start at $230.00 double

MELIA COZUMEL

www.meliacozumel.com
North Zone Beachfront
888-774-0040
All Inclusive 150 rooms
011-52-987-872-0700

This all-inclusive is located on a nice beach about 3 miles north of downtown. The room choices are standard and mini suites, with all rooms having terraces or balconies. Rooms are good sized and decorated in bright Caribbean style and colors. Club Fantasia provides musical entertainment and Mexican shows in the evening, fun for all. The food at this all inclusive gets good marks, and the reservation only restaurant, Café Paraiso serves up excellent steaks and seafood. There is a choice of 2 pools, one with a swim up bar. In addition to the usual tennis and non motorized water sports offered at all an inclusive, the Melia also offers horseback riding and Spanish lessons.

Rates start @ $95.00 pp. all inclusive

OCCIDENTAL GRAND

www.grandcozumel.com
South Zone Beachfront
800-858-2258
011-52-987-872-9730
ALL INCLUSIVE 252 rooms

Located on fabulous San Francisco Beach, with the lush Caribbean jungle set behind it, it is a beautiful property. The grounds are exceptionally manicured and groomed. The large standard rooms are simply but elegantly furnished and decorated, with all the amenities. The walk-in showers have plenty of room to hang dive gear, and still have room to shower. The AI food at the buffets is pretty much the same as other AIs, but their other restaurants are very good, be sure to try Los Olivos.

Consider renting a car unless you plan to spend all your time at the hotel.

It is a $20–$25 cab ride into town.

Rates start @ $230.00 double

PARK ROYAL

www.parkroyalhotels.com.mx
South Zone near Puerta Maya
888-774-0040
ALL INCLUSIVE 348 rooms

Park Royal Cozumel offers elegant, comfortable and spacious rooms and suites, all of them provided with private balconies. Rooms are nice size and come with all the normal amenities. Buffets are run of the mill AI, fine for the kids, but adults should stick to the reservation only restaurants for dinners. Breakfast buffets are good. This Cozumel property has three formal restaurants (Italian, Mexican, Caribbean) and one buffet restaurant; several bar areas; a beach area; an outdoors theater for nightly shows; and two pool areas.

Rates $161–$329 all inclusive

PLAYA AZUL HOTEL
www.playa-azul.com
North Zone Beachfront
011-52-987-872-0033

This is the only hotel in Cozumel that offers free greens fees at the golf club. They have some great golf packages. All rooms are oceanfront with large balconies to view the beautiful ocean. Suites, master suites, and a 3 bedroom garden house are all decked out in bright Mexican colors and furnishings. The hotel has a small sparsely populated sandy white beach and offers some good snorkeling. Be sure to try the fajitas in the on-site band and dancing right next door at the beach restaurant.
Rates $130–$350 double

PRESIDENTE-INTER-CONTINENTAL
www.cozumel.intercontinental.com
cozumel@interconti.com
South Zone Beachfront
888-303-1758
011-52-987-872-9500

Located on a beautiful white beach to the south of San Miguel, this lovely property is first class all the way. Beach and beachfront pools are a nice place to enjoy a day in the Caribbean, as the waiters serve your every wish.
Rooms are very large, understated and elegant. All rooms have balconies or terraces overlooking the ocean. At night you can see the twinkling lights from the mainland. There are three dining choices at the hotel, but the best is Alfredo's, which is gets rave reviews, even from the local chefs.
Rates $176–$595 double

VILLA & CONDO RENTALS

AT HOME IN COZUMEL
www.cozumel.tc
800-833-5971

This company offers only oceanfront properties." LOWEST PRICE GUARANTEE". They promise to meet or beat any lower price. The price must be for the same property, same dates, and for the same number of guests

COZUMEL HOMES.NET
www.cozumelhomes.net
830-928-3665
011-52-1-987-876-0835

This is a locally owned and operated business. Kelly has lived on the Island for many years and is a Mexican citizen. Let her assist you to find your perfect home away from home.

COZUMEL INSIDER PROPERTY RENTAL
www.cozumelinsider.com/proprentals
011-52-987-869-0504

They have a small selection of villas and condos. Especially popular are the "Isla Mar Vacation Villas". Often they have properties not listed.

COZUMEL PARADISE VILLAS
www.cozumelparadisevillas.com
800- 224-5551
303- 442-7644

Although this company is located in the USA they do have an office and staff on the Island for 24 hour service.

COZUMEL VACATION VILLAS
www.cozumel-villas.com
800-224-5551

They have a wide assortment of oceanfront, beach, and in-town properties.

ENJOY COZUMEL
www.enjoycozumel.com
507-281-0961
011-52- 987-869-0526
They handle both vacation and longer term rentals. It is also a locally based operation.

GO COZUMEL
www. gocozumel.com/vacation-rentals.htm
877-462-6986

I have seen lots of discounts on this site. If you do not find what you want then give them a call.

OTHER VILLA RENTAL WEB SITES:

www.idealvacationrentals.com

www.ivponline.com

www.realadventures.com

www.rent101.com

www.rentalscozumel.com

www.vacationhomes.com

Note: The same villas will be offered on several sites, check around for the best deal on a particular villa. It is also sometimes better if you lease through the company that actually does the property management in Cozumel for that property.

A SAMPLE LISTING OF VILLAS AND CONDOS

CASA BONITA - In town property. 3-bedroom/3 bath, AC, Cable TV, sleeps 6, no pool. $450–$650

CASA MARCOS - In town. 3-bedroom/1family room, 2-½ bath, AC, Cable TV, Phone, BBQ, Pool/patio/palapa. Sleeps 10-11. $975–$1400

PUESTA del SOL CONDOS - Water front north. 3 bedroom, 2 bath, AC, Satellite TV, VCR, Internet access, Pool, phone. $1300–$2400

VILLA RANAS SUR - Ocean front south. It has 10 bedrooms, 10 baths, beach, phone, TV, private pier. $7350–$8750

ISLA MAR VACATION RENTALS - A choice of 5 beautifully decorated vacation villas accommodating from 2 - 6 people in each. A wonderful alternative to hotels - Isla Mar Vacation Villas have full kitchens, maid service, pool, dive rinse and storage and way more ... From $68/day, $476/week + Packages Available Contact Sherri Davis at Cozumel Insider.

This is only a very small sample of what is available on the island. It is best to check the websites I have listed. Get on the discussion boards and ask for reviews from others who have stayed at a property you are interested in. Renting your own place, whether a studio apartment, or the largest villa on the island, is a wonderful experience.

Friday afternoon hangout for local expatriates!

CHAPTER IV

GETTING AROUND COZUMEL

Auto-Bus-Taxi-Bike

Depending on where you are staying and what you plan to do, there are several options for getting where you want to go. If you are staying downtown, a rental car is not necessary on a daily basis, although you may want to rent for one or two days, in order to visit the east side beaches and ruins.

You can walk to many of the best restaurants, shopping, dive piers, even the museum. For places a little too far for your stamina, taxi fares are very reasonable. (See list of fares.) There is also a network of vans and small busses called collectivos. This service is used mostly by the locals but can be used by anyone. Their destinations are listed on the side or front window and you can get on or off at any stops in-between.
Cost is seven pesos.

Bicycles are another fun option and are especially great for exploring the local neighborhoods and finding those hidden little shops and restaurants Bikes can be rented by the day or week, or bring your own if you are staying awhile. Better yet, buy one and give it to a child when you leave.

Scooters are available from several car rental operations at an average cost of $25 per day. This is the one form of transportation we do not recommend. There are and have been frequent injuries and fatalities to both locals and tourists. If you rent a car, please watch for the mopeds, they are sometimes hard to spot.

Car rentals are available from many places at many different prices. Both major chains such as Avis and National are there, and there are several good local choices as well. Shop on the Internet, send emails, and bargain during slow season. Be clear what your agreed upon price includes, some will include insurance, for others it is additional. Speaking of insurance, unless you have A LOT of cash or available credit, take the extra insurance. If you have an accident in Mexico, whether it is your fault or not, and there are damages, you could land up in jail. At the very least you will not be allowed to leave until fault has been decided and payment is made.

Rental vehicles range from the topless VW bug to a full size van. Be sure to check and document prior damages before accepting the vehicle. Also be aware that parking is limited, it best to use the parking lots that charge a few pesos and walk around. If you park on a red curb you may be towed, or your plates removed, and you will have to pay to get the car or the plates back.

When driving in Cozumel avenues have the right of way. Calles stop at every corner except where there is two-way traffic. The green light on the stoplight flashes when it is getting ready to change. Juarez separates the town into North and South. Even numbered Calles are on the North side and odd numbered Calles are on the South side. Right turns are usually permitted at a red light.

A warning about scooters

It should be mentioned that the majority of traffic accidents that befall tourists involve scooters (known locally as «motos»). These accidents seem to be due to a few factors:

Some inexperienced riders expect that if they can drive a car, then they can drive a scooter.

Some riders are unfamiliar with driving practices and conditions in Mexico.

Roads are not always in the best condition, and potholes are generally unmarked.

Scooters offer substantially less protection from accidents than anything with four wheels.

Tourists having too many alcoholic drinks and then driving "motos" also cause many accidents.

Scooters can be a great way to explore the island, but should only be driven by experienced riders, and even then only with extreme caution.

CAR RENTALS

ALAMO   1-800-462-5266
www.alamo.com
Maritime terminal
Puerto Maya
Downtown

AVIS   1-800-331-1084
www.avis.com
Airport   011-52-987-872-0219
Downtown   011-52-987-872-1923 ½ block off plaza

Fiesta Americana   011-52-987-872-9600
Maritime terminal   011-52-987-872-0094

BUDGET   1-800-472-3325
www.budget.com
Airport
Downtown Ave 5 between Calle 2 & 4

EXECUTIVE
rentacar@executive.com.mx
Airport
Downtown Calle 1 between Ave 5 & 10
011-52-987-872-1308

Ask for Julio and say Tony Rome sent you. You may get a nice discount.

HERTZ   1-800-654-3030
www.hertz.com
Downtown Ave 15 & Calle 10
Puerto Maya Pier
Punta Langosta
Maritime terminal
Hertz is also offering the battery operated Smart cars for rent.

LESS PAY   1-888-829-8084
www.islacozumel.net/services/lesspay
Downtown #628 Melgar Ave @ Barracuda Hotel
Park Royal Hotel   011-52-987-872-4744

MARLIN   011-52-987-872-5501
www.gocozumel.com/marlin
Downtown Ave 10 between Calle 2 & Juarez

NATIONAL 1-800-227-3876
www.nationalcar.com
Downtown

RENTADORA ISIS   011-52-987-872-3367
www.islacozumel.net/services/isis
rentadoraisis@prodigy.net.mx
Downtown Ave 5 between Calle 2&4

This is the author's choice when-ever I need a car. Margarita started this business as a young woman and with her honesty and great prices she has survived and grown. This is the only place I know that includes insurance and still has prices below the others. Call Margarita, you won't be sorry.

Tell her Patricia sent you! **Enjoy a 10% discount with the coupon from this book.**

SMART CAR   011-52-987-872-5651
www.gocozumel.com/smartcar
Across from Airport Ave 65
Downtown Calle 1 & Ave 10
Across from Puerto Maya Pier @ Pemex station

THRIFTY   1-800-847-4389
www.thrifty.com
Airport
Downtown
Note: If you receive a good deal arranged on the Internet, please bring copy of your confirmation or email, as sometimes the local agent will say they do not have such a rate. If you have the paper confirming they will not argue.

WARNING: *There have been recent incidents involving tourists being held until they paid for "lost wages" of persons injured in accidents. Be aware that even with insurance you can be held responsible for this. Also request a copy of the insurance you purchase stating exactly what and how much is covered.*

BICYCLE RENTALS

REN TAD O RA GALLO   011-52-987-869-2444
www.tourswilltravel.com
cozumelrental@yahoo.com.mx
Ave 10 #25 directly behind the Plaza building

They offer a large assortment of bikes for rent. Rentals include safety gear. $10 per day with weekly and monthly discounts. They also rent scooters and cars.

SOMBRERO RENTALS   011-52-987- 869-1519
www.sombrerorentals.com
Ave 10 Between Calle 2 & Juarez

This shop offers a good variety of both bikes and scooters. They take siesta from 1PM to 4 PM then stay open until 7 PM.

MOTOCARROS DE COZUMEL 011-52-987 857 0090
www.tuktukrental.com

This is something you have to see! Tuk-Tuks are 3 wheeled scooters with a top and seats for three people. I always see people out with them and it looks like they are enjoying themselves.

Note: Many of the hotels, vacation villas, and B&Bs offer free use of bikes to their rentals. Inquire about this when making your reservations.

PUBLIC PARKING LOTS

I am listing the lots in the Centro area from Ave 15 to Melgar, and Calle 7 to Calle 6. Hours are shown where they were listed, but most are open from 8am-9pm or 10pm. Price ranges from 7 pesos to 10 pesos per hour, and some discounted for scooters. There are new lots added often.

Ave 15 between Calles 2 & 4 8-11
Ave 15 between Calle 1 & Juarez 7-9:30
Ave 15 Between Calle 1 & Salas

Ave 10 between Calle 3 & Salas 8-11
Ave 10 between Salas & Calle 1 8-10
Ave 10 between Juarez & Calle 2

Ave 5 at Calle 6
Ave 5 between Calles 2 & 4
Ave 5 between Calles 3 & 5

Calle 4 between Ave 5 & 10

Calle 3 between Ave 10 & 5
Calle 3 between Ave 5 & Melgar across from Sorrissi
Calle 3 between Ave 5 & Melgar Plaza Orbi

Calle 5 between Ave 5 & Melgar

Calle 1 between Ave 10 & 15 7-10

There are others I am sure. Look for the words "estacionamiento público"

Also remember there is a lot behind Punta Langosta Mall if you can find a spot.

TAXI FARES

All fares are approximate due to the fluctuation in the exchange rates. Be sure to agree on the fare before getting in, or ask driver to see the fare schedule. Despite the established taxi fares, some cab drivers have begun charging double or even triple these rates. Be firm on a price before getting into the car. Most hotels post a list of standard cab fares or can give you advice on prices. Try to have the correct change or close to it, as some drivers will tell you they cannot make change. Prices are subject to change.

TIP Always ask the driver "how much" before getting in the taxi.

From Punta Langosta Pier:

Downtown $4 El Presidente Hotel $7 Mercado $5
Palmar Estate $6 Fiesta Americana $8 Chankanaab Park $10
Playa corona $11 Cozumel Country Club $10 Chen Rio Beach $21
San Clemente Beach $13 Mr. Sanchos $15 Playa Bonita $24
San Francisco Beach $13 Nachi Cocom $15 Punta Sur $30
North Hotel Zone $8 Palancar Beach $20 San Gervasio $45 rt
Playa Azul $8 Punta Morena $19 Paradise Beach $13
Puerto de Abrigo $6 El Cozumeleno $8 Ranch Las Palmas $15
Melia $8 Club del Sol $7 Airport $9
Puerta Maya Pier $6 Playa Mía Beach $15 Punta Francesa $18

From Puerta Maya Area:

El Presidente Hotel $6 Mercado $6
Palmar Estate $7 Fiesta Americana $7 Chankanaab Park $10
Playa corona $10 Cozumel Country Club $15 Chen Rio Beach $25
San Clemente Beach $12 Mr. Sanchos $14 Playa Bonita $30
San Francisco Beach $12 Nachi Cocom $14 Punta Sur $30
North Hotel Zone $12 Palancar Beach $17 San Gervasio RT $45
Playa Azul $12 Punta Morena $25 Paradise Beach $13
El Cozumeleno $8 Ranch Las Palmas $5 Melia $12
Airport $12 Playa Mia Beach $14

From Downtown:

Within downtown $2 El Presidente Hotel $6 Mercado $2
Cozumel Palace $4 Fiesta Americana $6 Chankanaab Park $9
Playa Corona $11 Cozumel Country Club $5 Chen Rio Beach $15
San Clemente Beach $14 Mr. Sanchos $13 Allegro $17
San Francisco Beach $14 Playa Bonita $18 North Hotel Zone $5
Palancar Beach $20 San Gervasio $45rt
Playa Azul $5 Paradise Beach $11 Reef club $12
Casa Del Mar $4 Ranch Las Palmas $8 Melia $5
Puerta Maya Pier $6 Playa Mía Beach $13 Iberostar $17

Taxis anywhere off the main drag to anywhere back in town are $18 pesos. A taxi that is flying a red flag is working in town and not on Melgar. They switch days so everyone gets to work Melgar. Taxis with no numbers have had their license taken away from them and will not stop for you. Rates may increase as the Taxi Union has requested a raise in fares.

Cozumel liquid gold.

CHAPTER V

DINING IN COZUMEL

EAT FOR $2.00 OR $100.00

DINING IN COZUMEL

The wide array of dining choices is amazing for such a small island with only one town. There is so much to choose from, everyone can be satisfied from the pickiest child to the gourmet snob. There are over one hundred dining establishments on Cozumel, but I have only listed those that I have either had experience with, or someone I know has patronized. I also am listing a few of the chain restaurants without reviews, after all, what more can be said about Pizza Hut or McDonalds.

To really savor the true taste of the Mayan Yucatan you must dine at a few of the small local Taquerias and Cocina Economicas (lunch on the run), it is at these small establishments that you will get a real sample of how the locals eat. The ethnicity of the food on the island is very diverse, Mexican, Mayan, American, Asian, Argentinean, French, and more. If you are looking for something particular, just ask on one of the discussion boards, someone will know.

Restaurants open and close here every year, but the majority have been around for some time. Many times a new establishment is only a new name, as often a chef or partner will venture out on his own to open a business, after cooking elsewhere for years. If you come across a restaurant that is not listed in this book, by all means please try it out and then let us know about it.

Please be aware that sometimes a taxi driver will tell you that a restaurant is closed or no longer exists. This is usually a ploy to direct you to another dining establishment where he will then get a bonus for delivering you to them. If this should happen to you, insist that you be taken to that address or get out and use another taxi.

Many of the restaurants have home delivery. If you see "servicio a domicilio" that means you can order by phone and they will deliver to you.

Bon Appetite!!

ECONOMICAL

3 PATITOS EMPANADAS
Ave 30 and Calle 15
No CC

The only items on the menu are fried *empanadas*. They usually have chicken, beef (ground meat), cheese, potato and bean. You can get your order to go or eat standing at the front counter. The *empanadas* are tasty and definitely worth the price. A lunch of 4 *empanadas* and a Coke before the tip is about $30 pesos.They are open mornings and afternoons.

ASADERO EL POLLO
Juarez Ave and Ave 30
They close when they run out of chicken…it can be as early as 3pm or as late as 7pm. Prices are inexpensive at 80 pesos. The grilled chicken is really yummy, and it comes with bags of rice, salsa, onions, and lots of corn tortillas. The chicken is grilled over a wood burning fire.

BACIO GELATERIA
987-872-6505
Melgar and Calle 3
7am-11pm

HMMMMMM, Genuine Italian gelato in every flavor you can imagine. A super treat on a hot day of walking. My baby grandson Dallas is already hooked. They also serve some pretty good coffee.

BOB'S COZUMEL
987-113-8678
www.facebook.com/BOBsCozumel
On the Square directly down from the ferry pier just past 5th Ave on the left side

Visit this great place for one of the BIGGEST beers on the island or one of their other refreshing signature adult beverages. Be sure and try the (quickly becoming) famous Italian Melt sandwich with a side of home-made fresh daily Pasta Salad, you won't be sorry you did! Come be your own Judge. This is becoming the "IN" place to meet and mingle. **Bring your coupon from "Cozumel the Complete Guide II" and receive a Free (w/purchase) souvenir shot glass of your choice.**

CAMERON DORADA RESTAURANT
987-872-7287
Juarez (cross island rd.) and Ave 105
7am-4pm

They serve seafood and pork dishes here but the most popular item is the Shrimp tacos. Two or three of these will easily fill you up. If you like really "HOT" stuff, ask for their special habanero salsa. Beware; because it is not just hot… it is HOT.

CAMILLO'S
987-872-6161
Ave 5 between Calles 2 & 4
VC/MC
This inexpensive seafood restaurant serves up the yummiest fried shrimp tacos at only 12 pesos each. This is dining, a very popular locals place. Dining room has AC. They offer Mexican style smoked marlin, ceviche, fillets, shrimp and lobsters.

CAREYCITO'S
Ave 65 between Calles 2&4
NO CC open 7pm–11pm

A great place to stop in and have an evening snack of Salbutes (small tortillas with a variety of toppings), or some tasty Panuchos (tortillas filled with beans and topped with lettuce, tomatoes, onions, and meat)

CASA DENNIS (counter in the back) not the main dining area.
Calle 1 just off the plaza
987-872-0067
NO CC Lunch only

Go all the way to the back and you will find a window with 2 women inside cooking. They have an assortment of snacks such at empanadas for less than $1. I often have lunch here for under $3.

CHILANGOS
Ave 30 between Calle 3 & Morelos
NO CC 6 pm–1am
You have only two choices to pick from here, both delicious, quesadillas and huaraches (folded over tortillas). Choose your toppings and fillings from behind the glassed in case, just point as needed. A favorite here is the nopales, which is cactus, very good, give it a try.

CHINA EXPRESS
987-869-0433
Closes around 5 PM
Salas between Ave 5&10

They have take-out and delivery only. I ordered sweet and sour chicken, fried rice, and an egg roll. Everything was delicious and cost me only $30 pesos

THE COFFEE (formerly known as the Coffee Bean)
Calle 3 between Melgar & Ave 5
NO CC 8 AM – 11 PM
You will feel at home as you walk in the door. Enjoy the aromatic smell of roasting coffee as you enter this little slice of Americana. They offer many tempting treats to indulge in. In addition to the various textures and flavors of coffee, tea, and "real" milkshakes, there is quiche, cakes, brownies, cookies, and assorted pastries in super-sized servings. Great place to relax with some friends or to use their free Wi-Fi.

DEL MUSEO
Waterfront @ Museum
NO CC B,L,D

Basic good food made even better by the setting and view. Sit out on the balcony overlooking the waterfront and enjoy the cool Caribbean breeze.
Especially popular at breakfast.

DEL SUR EMPANADAS ARGENTINAS
987-101-7108
delsur.empanadasargentinas@gmail.com
Ave 5 and Calle 3

This quickly became one of my favorite places for a snack or light meal. These empanadas are not what you would expect in Mexico. They are Made of special dough and filled with all kinds of mouthwatering flavors The tomato, basil, and cheese are my favorite, but they are all excellent. They also deliver if you desire. Rene is the owner and chef and is a pleasure to speak with. Since changing locations his menu has expanded to steaks and other food from the grill. His following expanded along with his menu and you may have to wait for a table. Tell him Patricia his muffin baker sent you.

DIEGO'S TACOS
65 Ave across from the airport
Behind car rental buildings

All I can say is YUMMY! They have awesome shrimp tacos here made with big shrimp and not those tiny shrimp. Good pork tacos and he even offers lobster tails at times if you ask. My family likes to check in at the airport and then go to Diego's to eat.

EL FOCO
Ave 5 Sur 13B
Between Rosado Salas and Calle 3
L&D
This is a small hole in the Wall that opens after 5pm. Their specialty is tacos, but their soups and other ítems are great too. Order one of the El Foco specials for about $8 and it will feed 2 people.

EL MERCADO
Salas between Ave 20–25
NO CC B,L,&D

This is not just one eatery, but at least 5 small open-air restaurants around the Mercado. They get crowded at breakfast with locals and visitors who know how to stretch their food budget. I have eaten breakfast at several of them and for under $3 U.S. I have had several excellent lunches here.

EL PERRO VERDE
987-117-7428
Ave 5 between Calles 3 & 5
B&L

Vegetarian visitors can stop at the casual, vegetarian El Perro Verde.Open only for breakfast and lunch, the cafe is famous for its chicken mole, Spanish omelet and Crazy Monkey sandwich, made with pumpkin seeds, celery and homemade peanut butter. Freshly mixed shakes, fruit juices and coffees also are available I am a meat and potatoes gal, but I have enjoyed some of their treats.

EL PIQUE
Ave 30 & Juarez
NO CC opens at 7pm
A local taqueria serving Tacos al Pasture and gringas, which are Tacos al Pasture with added cheese. 5 or 6 of these at 5 pesos apiece plus a coke and you have dinner for under $3.50.

EL SITO TACOS
987-876-1558
Calle 2 between Ave 10 & Ave 5
NO CC 7 am-noon

Be adventures and eat breakfast like a local. Serving some of the best seafood tacos and sandwiches in town. If you cannot accept eating this for breakfast then get them to go and take them on the boat or to the beach for your lunch.

EL TRIUNFO ROSTICERIA
Ave 30 & Calle 4
10am-5pm

This is another roasted chicken place cooking over the wood fire. You can buy ¼, ½, or a whole chicken. It also comes with side dishes and tortias. They do sometimes sell out before closing time.

FERVIC PASTELERIA & PIZZARIA
987-564-0815
Calle 11 between Ave 50 & 55
NO CC

The cakes and pastries coming out of this shop are incredible. They serve a tres leche cake that is to die for. They take orders for custom made birthday and wedding cakes. They recently added homemade pizza to the menu, try some and let me know how it is. You can also find them on Face Book now.

GIRASOLES
Calle 11 & Ave 45
987-869-1832
B, L

I go here for breakfast. Good food, moderate prices. What I like is I hardly ever see tourists there, although some must visit as their menu is available in English. Great eggs with green sauce and wonderful juice, makes for a great start to your day.

GRAND SLAM
Ave 30 across from Dominos
NO CC

A local torta eatery serving a torta special for $2.25 U.S. It is a combination of pulled pork, ham, cheese, grilled onions, letchuga, and avocado on a French roll. Eat one of these and you are set until dinnertime.

HOG TOWN CAFÉ
www.papahogs.com
987-872-1652
Melgar 2miles south of town

Margaret and Mike do as great a job on their food as they do with their divers! They serve up some terrific breakfasts to start your dive day. Then for lunch or a snack they cook up an assortment of burgers and sandwiches, Mexican dishes, and spaghetti. Check out their menu at their web site.

IL GIARDINO
Ave 15 between Calles 17&19
12-6pm
Each Sunday they make their special lasagna which is better than mine, and my lasagna is famous in my family.. The price for their lasagna is 60 pesos. Their usual selections are pasta, pork, chicken, shrimp and salad
dishes. You will be pleased with a very inexpensive bill.

LA CALETA DEL TIO JOSE
987-869-0124
Carretera Costera Sur Km 2.3
Near the light house south of town.
11:00 am – 8:30 pm

This is another new addition to Cozumel that is quickly becoming popular with both Mexican and Expatriate locals. They have some great cervesa and drink specials with 2 for 1 mixed drinks from 5-7. They have inexpensive offerings on the menu, with free salsa and chips from 11-5. Listen to an awesome guitarist each evening 5 pm to closing, while you enjoy that beautiful Cozumel sunset. **Get your first margarita free with our coupon found in the back of this book.**

LA CANDELA
987-878-4471
Ave 5 & Calle 6
NO CC 8am-6pm

This place is jam packed with locals by midafternoon. Serving homemade Yucatan food worth far more than the $45 pesos they charge. For that price you get a choice of soup, choice of 3 entries, which change daily, rice or spaghetti, and veggies or potatoes. Also comes with a cold drink of Jamaica (a tea made from hibiscus). Be sure to try the chicken cutlet stuffed with ham if it is available. They also serve a good breakfast, and it is one of my favorite places to start the morning.

LA COZUMELENA

Ave 10 & Calle 3

NO CC 7am-6pm

They have their own bakery on site for fresh bread and pastries. Serving both Mexican and American style breakfast. My large group of teens had no complaints and ate everything in sight. They have their own bakery adjoining the dining room. The smells coming from there are enough to cause you to gain 10 pounds. Pick up a pastry on your way out.

LA CUCINA ITALIANA

987-872-2730

Calle 6 between Ave 10&15

VC/MC

Literally translated as «the Italian Kitchen», this restaurant is owned and operated by the Tarroni Family, migrants from the Old Country. They have updated their Venetian dishes with a hint of the Caribbean. In this small comfortable dining room, you will be served a variety of homemade pastas, veal, chicken and seafood entrees prepared in the Northern Italian tradition. A slice of rum cake is the perfect way to top off your meal.

LA HACH

987-869-8403

Melgar across from Villa Blanca

Enjoy some good food and good drinks, at good prices. They have subs, sandwiches, and Mexican snacks. Frozen drinks are 2 for 1 all day at only $5, no tourist prices here. Happy Hours are 11-1 and 5-7. Relax and check out the beautiful sunsets, one of the best spots on the island. Say Hi to Alex and Sam(Samantha) for me. They also have a band several nights a week and I hear they rock the house. **Present our coupon and receive 15% off your bill. Not available during happy hours.**

LA HERRADURA

987-872-7754

Ave 30 between Calle 17 & 19

NO CC   12pm-5pm and 7pm-11pm

They serve comida corrida until 5:00 and then they re-open at 7:00 with a full menu including Pizza, Italian, Seafood, pastas and Chinese Food as well as Mexican food. This is the best pizza I have had on the island. I just love that they are only around the corner from me. Here is a little secret from Mike. If you want to try something other than pizza for dinner or comida corrida here, and have a special request you can place this a few days in advance and return for a one of a kind cooked meal that you create. He recommends a spicy tangy honey glazed Ahi Tuna that is served Cantonese style over rice,. They also deliver. **Receive a 15% discount with our coupon from 7-11 pm, dine in only.**

LA PARRILLA MISSION
www.laparrillamission.com
30th Avenue between Calles 2&4
987-869-2463
VC/MC/AMX   B,L,&D

Meat and pork chop tacos, frijoles churros, and salsa bar. Steaks are good and the price is right. I once fed 10 people for $78 including beer and soda. They do home delivery.

LA PERLITA
987-872-3452
Ave 65 between Calle 8&10
MC/VC 8 AM – 9 PM

Ceviche and fried fish are the main stays at this neighborhood restaurant and seafood market. Crowded with locals and families, definitely worth a taxi ride to sample their delicious fish.

LAS FLAMITAS
Ave 25 between Calle 3 & Morelos
NO CC

Here is another terrific Cocina Economica with a big bang for your Peso. No English spoken, but it is worth the effort to eat here. $3–$5 gets you soup, entrée, and drink, with a choice of 5–6 entrees daily. The Sopa de Lima is highly recommended. It is the best Yucatecan food on the island.

Las de Guanatos
Carretera Costera sur km 3.5
Across from Casa del Mar

Very economical, very tasty, and the cocktails... EXCELLENT. The de aguachile is great and the ceviche to drool for. After snorkeling from the beach in front of the restaurant, margaritas and cold beers are a great idea. The service is very friendly and they have all kinds of things in the menu.

LONCHERIA LAS PALMAS
Ave 25 & Calle 3
NO CC Lunch/Dinner

This is a very popular dining place for the locals. Daily specials include soup, entrée, and drink for $4.50 U.S. A bit more expensive, but still cheap is the shrimp brochette, a grilled shrimp dish that is outstanding.

LOS GARANONES
987-869-1646
Calle 11 between Ave 40&45
Across from sports field ,NO CC

These guys are fairly new on the block, but have quickly gained a following of both locals and tourists. Serving the traditional Mexican fare of tacos, fajitas, and other yummy dishes. You will not have to break your piggy bank to dine here.

LOS SERAS TAQUERIA
Ave 30 & Morelos
NO CC 7pm - 1am

They serve some of the best tacos Al Pastor on the island. $4.5 pesos per taco. Two people can eat for $6-7 U.S. including cokes. They also serve pizza and it in no way compares to Dominoes. Try the Al Pastor pizza for a real flavor treat.

MIDORI
987-869-3093
Ave Rosado Salas between Ave 10&15

This is a great place to go for both sushi and other scrumptious meals. I love the shrimp Tempura and the chicken curry. Prices are low and you get plenty to eat.

NINO'S PIZZA 2 LOCATIONS
989-6042/872-416
Ave 10 & Calle 3
Ave 65 between Calle 21 & 25

Open long hours and they will deliver to your hotel or villa. I have only used the Ave 10 location, but it was the better Pizzas I have tried so far in Cozumel. Since I often brought teen boys, I used them at least once or twice a trip. A large pizza was approximately $9.00 U.S

OTATE'S
987- 869-1059

Ave 10 between Calle 3 & 5

This is a little place just a bit past the plaza. It is cheap and excellent. We fed 6 of us for $45 and we were all stuffed with tacos, gringas, pozole, and cervesa. Mostly Spanish speaking but they understand some and pointing at the menu works well. They also deliver.

PARRILA COZUMEL
987-120-0774

Ave 30 between Calles 19 & 21 next to OXXO

Thank you Tim, I would starve without you. Great sandwiches and chicken dinners and now he has added breakfast. I eat his French fries every day when I am home.... they are the best. Free and fast delivery is available.

PAPRIKA MEXICAN & CARIBBEAN CUISINE
Open 7AM to 11PM. 987-872-2404

Carretera Costera Sur Km 4.5

Close to Park Royal

This is probably one of the best breakfast options in Cozumel! They have a lot of choices and the fresh juices and smoothies are delicious. Everything is made fresh and the servings are sometimes enough for two. Try the Nambi fish. It is a wahoo filet with mango chutney and banana tostones w/ Caribbean salad for lunch or dinner.

PESCADERIA SAN CARLOS
987-872-7440

Ave 50 bis between Calle 3 & Salas

NO CC 7am-5pm

This is a popular local seafood place and it is often packed. Located in the garden of a local fish market, they serve the freshest and best priced fish dinners on Cozumel. The fish cannot get any fresher, as it is his own catch. Dinner for two, including 2 cervesa each, is less than $160 pesos ($16 U.S.).

Look for the yellow sign that says Pescadores (fish market).

THE PUB SPORTS BAR
987-872-1503

Ave 10 between Salas & Calle 1

1pm-12am weekends until 2am

This is a great little sports bar serving both Mexican and American food. They have a special of the day for $60 pesos at lunch. Karaoke can be enjoyed on many evenings.

ROCK'N JAVA THAI NOODLE BAR
011-987-869-2794
Downstairs from Mega on Melgar
VC/MC/AMX

This is a very small place seating about 20 people. They serve tasty Thai food at inexpensive prices. A great place for a quick lunch or maybe a take home dinner. They also deliver for those of us who are too lazy to venture out or away from the pool.

SABORES
Ave 5 between Calle 3 & 5
NO CC 11-5

Here is another popular cocina economica with home style Yucatan cooking. For about $5.00 you get soup, entrée, rice, veggie, and drink. Eat in the dining room, or enjoy your meal in the garden.

SUPER HIT I, II, & III
I   Ave 30 & Salas
II Ave 30 & 15
III Calle 11 between Ave 35 & 40

Three great places for tortas and other Mexican foods. Large, tasty, and awesome sandwiches are the main treat here. Try my favorite, the pork pibil with all the toppings. You can eat in or take out ("para llevar" said PAH-rah yey VAR). Very little English is spoken here, but you can point to the menu boards.

SUSHIE n' GO
987- 872-6509
Calle 11 between Melgar & Ave 5

They serve excellent sushi at affordable prices. All the usual choices such as "California roll' and "spicy tuna roll", but they also serve many originals. Try the "habanero roll". They also serve sub sandwiches. Prices range from $45 MP - $70 MP.

TAQUERIA DIAZ
Ave 30 between Juarez & Calle 2

Another little hole in the wall with great tacos. Lunch for 2 about $6.

TAQUERIA CORONADO
Calle 8 between Ave 30 & 35

Tacos for 7 MP and tortas for 15 MP. Hard to beat the price and the
food is good.

TONITA'S
Rosado Salas between Ave 10 & 15
NO CC B, L

Typical home style Yucatan cooking. The Pozole/Posole comes highly recommended
by friends. Tuesday is Chile Relleno day, get there early because they have the best
chiles rellenos on the island, and can run out quickly.

WOODY'S BAR & GRILL
north east side of the square next to the 7/11

This place is like a mini "Cheers". Inexpensive cervesa, burgers, and other quick
meals. Food is good and the prices are low. Another place the "locals" hang out.

ZERMATT BAKERY
Ave 5 and Calle 4
NO CC 7am-7pm

This is a super place for a quick breakfast or pick-me-up. Mouthwatering pastries, hard
rolls, and good coffee is what you will find here.. Sit outside at one of the sidewalk
tables, or buy a dozen and take them home. This has long been a favorite of both
locals and visitors alike.

MODERATE

AL PIE DEL CARBON
987-101-2599
Calle 6 & Ave 5

Now this is a genuine grill! Open flame cooking over real wooden logs. Grilled veggie on skewers and the beef is true Argentinean beef. The grilled fish is a treat and at a great price. Try the grilled veggie salad and the baked empanadas; neither is on the menu so you must ask for them

ALBINO'S
987-869-2510
Ave 20 between Calle 10 & 12
Noon to 8PM

Albino's is a breath of fresh air, the food is exquisite and so is the service. You will not be disappointed. It's not on the main street but is well worth the detour. If you want a "local" restaurant away from all the tourist joints, you will have a great experience.

BLUE ANGEL RESTAURANT
987 872 0819
2.3 Costera Sur, Cozumel
In the Blue Angel Resort
B, L, D

The food here is absolutely excellent. The chimichanga and chili rellenos are outstanding. Breakfast offers Mexican and American dishes plus the staff accommodates special requests. Lunch has a selection of authentic Mexican dishes as well as North American style sandwiches and burgers. In addition to the dinner menu, the restaurant offers theme nights. There are not many restaurants in Cozumel that offer such great ocean views

BUCANNO'S BAR & GRILL
www.clubcozumelcaribe.info/
987-872-0100
Club Caribe, Playa San Juan
North Hotel Zone I love this place. It is a super beach club with a large pool, nice beach, and good food. Prices are not cheap but neither are they overpriced. Servings are large and often can be shared. You may be charged a $10 entry if you are not a local but you will get the same in food and beverage credit.

CAMILLOS
Ave 5 between Calle 2 & 4
No cc

The seafood cocktail is the best. The stuffed avocado is superb. I also recommend any of the seafood tostadas and the fried fish fingers. The friendly staff and owner make you feel like family. If you can read Spanish ask for the Spanish menu. The English menu is in U.S. dollars using a 10 to 1 exchange.

CASA BLANCA
On the plaza at Calle 1 and Ave 5

This is personal favorite of the author's fussy Son. A terrific place to people watch, as it is right on the corner of the plaza. Serving many Yucatan specialties, but the nachos with chicken are really yummy and the serving is large. Don't forget to purchase the Casa Blanca souvenir, a painted tile with a Senor or Senorita and your name and Casa Blanca on it.

CASA DENIS
Calle 1 just off the plaza
987-872-0067
NO CC B, L, &D

This is the oldest restaurant on Cozumel and a longtime favorite of locals and visitors alike. A great place for people watching on the plaza, or listening to the strolling musicians. It is another favorite of the author and many local. There are too many terrific dishes to choose a favorite, they are open quite late.

CHEN RIO
East coast beach road
NO CC

One of the most popular beachfront restaurants on the East side, mostly for the beach location. Food is so-so, flies are annoying at times, but a fun place and serves a strong Margarita. Be sure to ask the prices before ordering, if the menu is recited and not shown to you. Some visitors love this place and I have heard you should order the seafood platter.

CHI
987-869-8156
www.chicozumel.com
Calle 3 & Melgar, above Pizza Hut
This seems to be popular with many locals. I have had a few of their Chinese and Filipino dishes and managed to enjoy every bite.. Their regular menu is reasonable and has Seafood, Chinese, and Philippino dishes. Owned and operated by the same family as Sam's Wok.

COCONUT'S
East side beach rd.
NO CC

Worth the visit for the awesome view alone. Set high on a cliff with a view of the beach and crashing surf. Enjoy a lunch of quesadias and a cold cervesa, or try the coconut shrimp hmmmm scrumptious. Bring a tee shirt from your hometown to add to the ceiling of the palapa roof. There is a small secluded cove just below, but be sure to check it ahead before taking children down.

CONCHITA del CARIBE
987- 872-5888
www.laconchitadelcaribe.com
Ave 65 between call 13 & 15
NO CC

Serving some of the best seafood on the Island for reasonable prices. The ceviche and seafood soup are both great to start a meal with, then have the catch of the day.

COSTA BRAVA
Calle 7, around the corner from post office
MC, V, AE   B,L,&D

I have never had a bad meal here, whether it was breakfast, lunch or dinner. I get the same report from other Cozumel frequent visitors. Breakfast for two including eggs, meat, beans, and coffee runs $6–7 U.S. The conch and the lobster also get high marks as does the Mexican platter for two. Bring them your catch when you fish, for $2 U.S. they will cook it up and serve it with side dishes.

DANUBE
miryam@danubecoz.com
Plaza i 95 across from Puerta Maya
987-989-6349 x107

Here comes the new kid on the block and it looks like Danube is knocking it out of the park. European dishes like pan-fried braised beef pierogies, falafel with grilled flatbread, shrimp and scallop ravioli, and coconut curry shrimp, and many dishes you will not find anywhere else on the island. I have heard that it is a MUST to save room for their citrus tart.

EL ABUELO GERADO
Ave 10 between Calle 2 & Juarez
B, L,&D

I have received mostly good reviews on this little place. This is another family run restaurant on Cozumel. El Abuelo Gerado is Spanish for Grandfather Gerard, the patriarch. Service is from early morning to late at night. I myself have had both good and bad service here. Considering the reviews, I suggest you give it a try. You can either dine in the back garden or in the dining room where you can people watch. The lobster is priced in the teens and I enjoyed it when I ordered it.

EL MORRO
Ave 75 between Calle 2 & 4
987-872-3029
MC. VC

A favorite of divers and locals, it has been discovered by tourists due to its excellent food, good prices, and frequent mention in guide books. It is a bit far from the center of town, but well worth the trip. Fresh seafood of all types, the seafood platter is huge and will feed two persons with average appetites. The giant Margaritas and pina coladas are good, but beware driving afterwards. Kids love the video games in the back.

EL TURIX
987-872-5234
Ave 20 between Calle 17 & 19
NO CC Dinner only

Located in a residential area serving Yucatecan dishes. A very simple establishment with excellent food and a friendly smiling staff. My favorite dishes here are the Panuchos (fried tortilla with chicken and avocado), and the chicken in black chili sauce.

ESPECIAS
987-876-1558
Calle 3 between Ave 5 & 10
Upstairs, no cc

World cuisine served in an intimate setting. A must visit while in Cozumel. Adrian is the owner and chef at this fantastic little place. He is a member of the Casa Dennis family and I think he was born cooking. Argentinean and Mexican dishes, his meals are of gourmet quality, how he serves these dishes at these low prices is a mystery. Everything is wonderful here, but be sure to try the empanadas and the crab fingers. My favorite is the shrimp stuffed with cheese and wrapped in bacon. Relax after dinner with drinks while you listen to the classical guitarists that play every evening. I recommend reservations during holidays and Carnaval, calling before you even get on the plane. **Our readers are offered a free appetizer with coupon.**

ERNESTO'S FAJITA FACTORY
987-872-1154
Melgar, oceanfront, just north of La Ceiba

This is your basic Tex-Mex, that said, it is terrific Tex-Mex. Serves some of the best shrimp nachos and fajitas I have ever eaten. Noisy and fun, beware of the tequila shooters.

FRATELLI'S
Ave 10 & Calle 8

This little Italian bistro is in the building that used to be Mr. Manati's. It seems they get mixed reviews. Some locals and visitors praise them and others say it is "too much for too little." If you like Italian give it a try and judge for yourself. The thin and crispy pizza seems to please everyone.

FRENCH QUARTER
987-872-6321
Ave 5 between Salas & Calle 3
V, MC, AE Dinner only

The Big Easy has arrived in Cozumel. Serving authentic New Orleans Cajun food. Specialty is the filet minion with red onion marmalade. Thejambalaya and etoufee is also good. Dine inside, or on the balcony.

HARD ROCK CAFÉ
987-872-5271
Melgar #2A, ½ a block north of ferry pier
www.hardrockcafecozumel.com
VC/MC/AMX

This is supposed to be the smallest Hard Rock Café in the world, but they may have lost that honor to their smaller location at Punta Langosta Mall. It is basically like every other Hard Rock but with a local touch of Mexican. When I am craving a true American cheeseburger, this is the place I go.

HC de MONTERREY RESTAURANT
987-872-2277
Ave 5 ½ block before Cemetery
NO CC   L&D

It is nothing special to look but well worth the trip. Go there for meat called Arrechera. There is national and international style. (Both are very good). Feel free to order off the menu but I recommend for 2 people is 1/2 kilo of national Arrechera meat with your choice of a baked onion, or baked potato along with salsa, crema, avocado, lime and fresh tortillas. Allows you to make the best tacos ever! Always packed full of people, it is also a good place to buy your meat for a BBQ at home. It is a butcher shop and restaurant. Just fantastic food.

JEANNIES WAFFLE HOUSE
Melgar & Calle 11
MC, V

Another favorite of divers for that early morning breakfast. Large Mexican and American breakfasts. Although I was not impressed, it is basically a Mexican IHOP, my picky teens were quite happy and ate everything, and it gets good reviews elsewhere. It is nice to eat here for the view alone. Please note that this is not the original Jeannie's.

KELLEY'S BAR & GRILL
kelleysbarandgrill@yahoo.com
Ave 10 between Calle 1 & Salas

After your first visit to Kelly's you will have found a home away from home. It is a favorite hangout of frequent visitors and expats who gather to tell "tall tales" and watch sports. Menu items include; chilidogs, Reuben's, giant burritos, and some other specialties you won't find anywhere else. How about some real Irish stew or some southern chicken fried steak with real mashed potatoes. Comfort food for when you are away from home too long. Gene has some of the BEST ribs around. **Bring in your coupon from this book and Gene will give you a free cervesa or Margarita.**

KINTA
www.kintacozumel.com
987-869-0544
Ave 5between Calle 2 & 4

All I can say here is "Kris take a bow please!" Kris Wallenta is one of the most original, inventive, and fantastic chefs I have ever met. This is "fine dining" at affordable prices. Take a date here and hide the bill, she will think you spent your paycheck. The menu is changed every 3 months so you will never get bored, as if you could. Kris blends his spices, cheeses and other ingredients into flavors one would never imagine. Be sure to save room for desert and try his Mexican version of Crème Brule. I am drooling while writing this**! Enjoy a glass of their tasty Sangria free with the coupon from "Cozumel the Complete Guide II".**

KONDESA
987-869-1086
Ave 5 between Calles 5 & 7

The Wallenta brothers Kris and Jason have hit another home run with this new dining experience. True Mexican cuisine with an upscale touch. Service is just as great as it is at Kinta. Once again a fine dining experience at moderate prices. The ambiance is sophisticated yet casual. Kondesa is sure to be as popular as its sister Kinta. **Enjoy a glass of their tasty Sangria free with the coupon from "Cozumel the Complete Guide II".**

LA CASA DEL HABANO STEAK & TAPAS BAR
987-876-1226
On Melgar across from the ferry pier

The Tuna Tartar is outstanding. The combination of tuna, avocado, mango and wasabi mayonnaise is just yummy. Be sure to try the oysters Rockefeller and the special rib eye quesadillas. You can't beat the view; it is right in front of the downtown ferry pier, and overlooking the square.

LA CHOZA
987-872-0958
Ave 10 between Calle 3 & Salas
MC, V B,L,&D

Serving from early morning to late evening, this is an excellent choice for any meal. Serves breakfast at low prices, has good lunch specials that locals are aware of, but the tourists need to ask about. Food is delicious and service is friendly.

LA MORENA
987-879-1923
Ave 10 between Calle 3 & 5

Excellent seafood and Mexican dishes, but the big draw here is the Mexican Coffee prepared at your table. Coffee, tequila, coconut ice cream, and cinnamon, simply delectable.

LAS TORTUGAS
987- 872-1242
Pedro Joaquin Coldwell (Ave 30) & Calle 19
Dinner only CC

The name translates to "The Turtles". This is a traditional Mexican restaurant, you will not find Tex-Mex here. Try the conch ceviche, I am told it is very good.

MARGARITAVILLE
www.margaritaville.com
Melgar & Calle 11
987-872-0278
VC/MC/AMX 9am-2am

This is the largest Margaritaville in Mexico. I hesitated to put this in the moderate section as it is really borderline depending on what you order. A cheeseburger with fries will run the $12 average that it costs in most touristy places like this. That being what it is, the food is decent and some things like the "pulled pork sandwich" are excellent. The place is lively and entertaining, particularly in the afternoons. My main problem with them is that even though it is a Jimmy Buffett operation, they do not play his music.

MOSAICOZ
987-872-6964
On the back of the Square

Mosaicoz can be tough to find, because it is in the restaurant gauntlet on the way to Casa Denis. This place has truly cheap beers, 12 pesos. They'll bring you complimentary chips and salsa. The salad is enough for 2 and they one of the best salads on the island. We get the wood fired «Belize» pizza with a very thin crust and lots of veggies and chicken. It can be enough for 2 people.

OHANA CAFÉ & BAR
www.ohanacozumel.com
Ave 5 between Calles 6 & 8
B, L, &D

This new place is getting rave reviews about their food, service, and entertainment. Live jazz, blues, and reggae can be heard from 8 to 11. I hear the "Coconut Shrimp" is now the best on the island. I plan on trying the "Lobster Burger". For breakfast the "Banana Pecan" pancakes with melted butter just make my mouth water.

OLIVE
Ave 5 & Calle 5

They have so many great things here that it is hard to choose. Olive and blue cheese tapenade, the seafood capriccio over mashed potatoes and the lobster and bacon sandwich just to name a few. I am not a wine drinker but those who are say they have the best wines on the island.

PALMERA'S
987-872-0532
Melgar in front of the ferry terminal
V, MC, AE   B, L, D

Can you say Denny's in Spanish! But then I actually like Denny's as do many other people. The food is pretty good and the fried fish I ate was extremely good. Get a street front table for breakfast and people watch as all the cruise ship tourists descend and the ferries unload. This is definitely the place for dinner during Carnaval, get there early and have a very long dinner, and a front seat for viewing the parades. **Palmera's is offering 15% off with the coupon from Cozumel the Complete Guide II.**

PLAZA LEZA
South side of the plaza

The food is good and the menu is long, but the company of Miguel is what brings me back. He is a perfect host, entertaining and friendly. Ladies, if the music is playing in the park ask him to "salsa" with you. OK, back to the food. International and Mexican dishes, steaks and seafood, and it is all good. If you don't see it on the menu, ask. It is a great place to sit and watch the band in the park.

ROCK'N JAVA
602 Melgar just past the mall
NO CC B, L

This is a longtime favorite of locals and tourists alike. They serve a good breakfast and very good salads. This is a good choice of dining for vegetarians. If you want to donate to the Humane Society, or drop off supplies for them, this is the place to do it.

ROLANDI'S
www.rolandis.com
Melgar Ave & Calle 11next to Margaritaville
987-872-1097

This newest edition to Cozumel has been long awaited by many visitors and locals alike. Located on the waterfront the view is stunning and reason alone to dine there. Rolandi's is a franchise and if you have dined in Playa del Carmen or Cancun you already know how good the food is. They have a long list of pizza types and a great pasta selection. In addition to that, they have many other choices. They also have a fairly wide wine selection. The only negative here is the overlapping music from Margaritaville, mainly in the afternoons.

SENOR FROG'S
www.senorfrogs.com/cozumel
Melgar @ Punta Langosta Mall
987-869-1650
VC/MC/AMX

This is again a repeat of what you will find at Carlos' N Charlie's, downstairs. Lots of music and lots of loud fun. Basic food is burgers and nachos. The one special thing here is my nephew Daniel who is the best MC around. I may be biased, but he will make sure you have fun. There is also a mini Frog's at the International Pier. It is called ½ **Senor Frogs** and has the same food, drinks, and fun, with the extra bonus of a beach and slide. This location is only for the cruise ships, unless you are diving with "Dive with Martin", as the shop is located at the pier.

SAM'S WOK
987- 857-1446
Across the street from Puerta Maya

Tasty Chinese food at reasonable prices. Frequented by the crews from the cruise ships, so you know it's good. A short stroll for anyone staying at El Cid or Park Royal.

SONORA GRILL
987- 872-3620
Juarez & Ave 15

Open for breakfast, lunch, and dinner, they feature Mexican cuisine. Enjoy sitting at the balcony and people watch while you eat.

TONY ROME'S EMBASSY RESTAURANT
987-872-0131
Ave 5 between Salas & Calle 3
NO CC Opens @ 3pm

Tony and his wife Maria Jose are your warm and friendly hosts for the evening. He has the BEST ribs in town, served with his own special sauce. My favorite is the Chicken Parmesan; no one else has it this good. No connection to the Tony Roma chain, but ask him to tell you that story, very interesting, and the ribs here are above and beyond any others I have had. The meat falls off and melts in your mouth. Other dishes are good too, but do not leave without a piece of either Key Lime pie, or Mango Pie. He will also cook your catch from that fishing charter. **Get 10% off with our coupon in the back of the book.**

WET WENDY'S
www.wetwendys.com
987-8724970
Ave 5 1 block north of the square

This is a great place with great margaritas, good food, and a fun staff. Owned and operated by a wonderful couple. It is like an adult ice cream shop, but the treats are the most imaginative margaritas in the world. Try the coconut peanut butter or the orange creamsicle, they are to die for. The food is also excellent and fairly priced. The burrito is big enough for 2 people. Lots of local expatriates will be found relaxing here. It is the only place you're going to find authentic, homemade, Hungarian Goulash

EXPENSIVE

AL CAPI NAVEGANTE
987-872-1730
312 Ave 10
V, MC, AE dinner only

This is primarily a seafood restaurant, although there are two chicken and steak dishes on the menu. Servings are large and the food is good. Meals are served in a very nice sea themed décor. Be sure to leave room for flambé desserts prepared at tableside.

AL FREDO di ROMA
987-872-0322
Hotel Presidente
V, MC, AX

Serving gourmet Italian and Mexican fare, this new addition is quickly becoming popular. A local owner and chef swears he will go broke from eating there so often. Their pasta is reasonable, and I am told it is outstanding.

ALBERTO'S BEACH BAR RESTAURANT
www.albertosbeachbar.com
987-102-8260 CELL
Carretera Costera Sur km 18

Alberto's Beach Bar and Restaurant is just a 5 minute walk down the beach from the Occidental Grand Hotel. Alberto's has great, fresh seafood!!! Staff is very friendly and welcoming. Seating is right on the beach, so it is a great place for dinner and watching the sunset! I would suggest the seafood plate for 2 which includes grilled shrimp, conch, maui maui, and lobster tail!

AMBARS
5 Av #141 between 1 and Rosado Salas
869-1955
Dinner only

Serving gourmet Italian fare in a romantic setting on the terrace. Nice place for that special date.

CASA MISSION
872-1641
Juarez & Calle 55
V, MC, AE

The main attractions here are the beautiful gardens. The fajitas seem to be the favorite menu item. Reviews of this establishment are mixed, so try it for yourself.

GUIDO'S
987-872-0946
#23 Ave Rafael E. Melgar
V, MC

Guido's is best known for their gourmet pizzas which are baked in wood burning ovens and their famous sangria. Be sure to get an order of the garlic bread, quite different from what we are accustomed to, but tastes awesome. To get away from the heat of the ovens, dine out on the patio, it is more romantic anyway.

LA COCAY
www.lacocay.com
987-872-4407
Calle 8 between Ave 10 & 15
V, MC L, D

This a perfect place to celebrate that birthday or anniversary. Gourmet Mediterranean cuisine such as tuna tartar with avocado wasabi mayonnaise for appetizer, and entrees such as almond and vanilla bean crusted fish of the day.

LA LOBSTERIA
Ave 5 & Calle 7
NO CC

This one of the best places for lobster in Cozumel. Gourmet salads with lobster are high on my list. There is a lot to try here with original recipes, using seafood, pasta and beef.

LA VERANDA

987-872-4132

Calle 4 between Ave 5 & 10

MC, V

This is probably the most romantic setting for a restaurant on the island. Try the shrimp Caribbean prepared and flamed at your table, or seafood salad for two ($38 U.S.).

LOBSTER HOUSE

NORTH HOTEL ZONE

NO CC dinner only

Serves the biggest lobsters they can find. Pick your own dinner out from the tank. A longtime favorite for lobster, nothing else is served here. Make sure that you bring mosquito repellent. Those critters are bad up on the north side.

PANCHO'S BACKYARD

www.panchosbackyard.com

Melgar Ave @ Los Cinco Soles

987-872-2141

V, MC, AE

Located within the Los Cinco Sole store, this is a popular establishment with tourists. Food is good and service is excellent. It is a nice place to have an elegant lunch after shopping.

PEPE'S GRILL

www.pepesgrillcozumel.com

Megar & Salas

987-872-0213

Definitely not for the economy minded, but a nice choice for a special night out. Ocean view dining and good food in elegant surroundings. I have heard that this is where the Bill Gates crowd dines when they are in port. Serving steaks and seafood, but for dessert try the orange crepes with Spanish coffee. **Use Pepe's coupon from this book and get 15% off that special dinner.**

PRIMA'S TRATTORIA

www.primacozumel.com
Melgar across from Palacio
987-872-6567
V, MC, AMX B/L/D

Italian pasta dishes, seafood, and the freshest salads in Cozumel are the order of the day here. This establishment is upstairs atop the El Cantil Condo. Dine inside or outside. Both offer a spectacular view of the water clear to the mainland. Enjoy people watching from the terrace while you eat. A very busy and popular place, you may have to wait for a table. **Albert is offering our readers a 10% discount with coupon on lunch** or dinner, holidays excluded.

SORRISI

www.sorrisicozumel.com
Calle 3 #317 between Melgar & Ave 5
987-869-0960/0961
When you enter this restaurant you will swear you have been transported to old Italy. The ambiance is almost seductive. Sorrisi 's owner and the entire Chefs crew are actually from Italy. Most of their supplies for your dinner are also imported from Italy. Meal choices range from basic pizza to gourmet dishes. The Sangria is some of the best I have ever tasted.

IF YOU MUST!!!

BURGER KING 3 locations: Ave 30
Punta Langosta Mall
Chedraui Mall

DOMINO'S PIZZA Calle 5 delivers 872-1635

MCDONALDS Melgar waterfront 881-7700

PIZZA HUT Melgar & Calle 5 delivers
872-5055/5056/5057

SUBWAY Calle 11 between Melgar and Ave 5
872-3678

DINING AT YOUR VILLA

If you have rented a casa or villa and have cooking facilities, you can save some vacation dollars and have some fun at the same time. Shop in the Mercado or the local grocery stores for food and supplies. Take some lessons in Yucatán cooking or just use a few of the recipes listed at the end. The Fruit, veggies, meat and fish on the island are fresh and will taste so good. Whenever I bring a group, we always have a poolside dinner party or BBQ at least once or twice…really a lot of fun and it stretches the budget.

SHOPPING FOR FOOD

MERCADO:
Ave 25 & Salas

The freshest fruit and veggies in town at the lowest prices are found here. Meats, poultry and fish also available, although it is hung in the open and it will depend how you feel about this.

CHEDRAUI:
At edge of town, near Melgar and Calle 11.

This is a Mexican version of a super Wal-Mart, stocking groceries, meats, produce, and of course all the non-food items. They also have beer and some liquor at decent prices, and a deli section.

MEGA COMMERCIAL MEXICANA
Melgar & Calle 11

This store is a mega-market with import and national food items, large meat, deli, and bakery departments, electronics, clothes, books, bakery, deli, household items and more.

PACSADELI
Ave 45 & Calle 2

A small shop that carries a lot of imports and items normally unavailable in Cozumel Carries assorted red meats, deli meats, canned goods, dairy products, and a large assortment of spices. This is where I find my "Stove Top Dressing".

SAN FRANCISCO MARKETS:
2 locations: Ave 30 & Juarez/Ave 65 & Calle 23
A Mexican supermarket compares, with American small Winn Dixie. There is a Deli in the store.

SEDENA:
Corner of Rafael Melgar &
Carlos A. Gonzalez F. (Airport Road)
987-872-0572

This is a small market, but often has things not found it the others. Has the best price on Vanilla in town. They also have a nice selection of Swiss Army knives and Multi-tools near the front entrance. Prices are good here on most everything.

SORIANA
Calle 8 Norte & Ave 30
987-872-4440

Another nice supermarket that often has things not available in the others. I often buy my meat here because the meat department is so clean and the meat is good. Repeat visitors will remember this store as "Super Maz".

HOME DELIVERY

Cozumel Chef
www.cozumelchef.com
Delivery and Chef service
987-105-5300
908-268-3228 USA

Cozumel Chef is a fine dining private cooking service that brings the restaurant to your vacation home. The chef is a classically trained chef from the French Culinary Institute in New York City. cozumelchef.com offers a variety of menus to choose from, each uniquely Mexican with a French technique twist Also available are delivery services for groceries and culinary tours.

COOKING SERVICE BY THE ESPINOZA SISTERS
987-119-8900 OR 987-117-2106

Reina and Veronica Espinoza will cook an excellent Mexican dinner for you and your guests. They charge $8 US plus the cost of groceries. They do the shopping, the cooking, and clean up afterwards. I have heard only good things about these ladies. Contact them for a copy of their menu. Everything from lobster to pazole is available.

TE LO LLEVAMOS
www.telollevamos.com.mx
Grocery Delivery to Condos and Villas
987-872-5200

Te Lo Llevamos will deliver groceries for a 10% markup and delivery fee (fee varies on location-el centro, north end, south end). You place your order at least a week or two in advance of arrival. Pay 50% up front and the balance when delivered with receipts. This is a great way to get right to the pool instead of shopping for food first.

Shopping tip:
Remember when ordering by weight that 1-kilogram is equal to 2.2 pounds.

COOKING LESSONS

COZUMEL COOKERY
talktous@cozumelmycozumel.com
Josephina's Kitchen

Each Class will cover the basics of Yucatecan cooking, including a desert. Then you have a choice of one main entree. Unless noted, all ingredients are covered in the cost of the classes. The class includes a trip to the market to learn how to pick out your ingredients. Prices are $69 pp. for 2-3 people, $79 pp. for 2-3 people, $68 for 4-8 people, and $59 for 8-12 and private lessons can be arranged for 1 person.

SAMPLE RECIPES FROM MEXICO

Tortilla Shrimp Grill

Ingredients:

4 Soft Taco Size Flour Tortillas
1 large cored and finely chopped Pineapple peeled
3 Tbsp. Cilantro chopped
1 Red Bell Pepper finely chopped
1 Green Bell Pepper finely chopped
1 small Red Onion finely chopped
2 Tbsp. Parsley chopped
1 Serrano Chile minced
1/2 cup Vegetable Oil
4 Tbsp. Lime Juice
20 ncooked, peeled and deveined shrimp

Combine the pineapple, peppers, onion, cilantro, parsley, chili and 1/2 of the oil and lime juice together in a medium glass bowl.

Season with salt and pepper to taste. Then chill for 50 minutes. Prepare the BBQ (High heat). Combine the remaining oil and lime juice together and add shrimp; toss to coat with marinade.

Grill until opaque, about 1 minute per side. Grill tortillas on each side for 30 seconds.

Place 5 shrimp onto each tortilla. Spoon on salsa and serve.

Ceviche

Ingredients:

2 pounds Cubed white fish, shrimp, or bay scallops, raw
5 - 10 Serrano peppers or jalapeño chiles (very hot), diced

1 Red bell pepper, diced
1 Green Chiles, diced
1-2 ripe tomatoes, diced

1-2 minced garlic
1 large diced avocado
1 bunch of cilantro with stems
1 tsp. sugar
2 cups lime juice
1 bag of tortia chips

In a large bowl combine all ingredients except 1/2 the avocado and cilantro. Toss gently but thoroughly, making sure all fish is coated with lemon-lime mixture. Cover and refrigerate for one to three hours, stirring occasionally. Fish should become quite white and scallops will lose translucent appearance. (Once this happens, you will know that the lime juice has cooked the fish).

Chicken Tamales

Ingredients:

6 cups corn mesa mix for tamales
6 cups chicken broth
1 cup vegetable oil
2 tsp. Salt
1 tsp. baking powder
1 1/2 large rotisserie chicken
2 cans salsa verde or tomatillo sauce
1 bag of corn husks

Soak the corn husks in warm water until soft. Blend with an electric mixer Maseca corn masa mix for tamales, corn oil, salt, baking powder and the chicken broth to obtain a consistent mixture. Shred the chicken and marinate in the green salsa or tomatillo sauce.

Spread masa evenly over corn husks, and spread a spoonful of marinated chicken on top of the masa.
Fold the sides of the corn husk to center over the masa so that they overlap to make along package.
Fold the empty part of the husk under so that it rest against the side of the tamale with a seam. Place the tamales in a steamer and cook tamales for 35-40 minutes. Check every 20 minutes. The tamales are cooked when they separate easily.

Mexican Fondue

Ingredients:

Tortilla
Chips
2 Tbsps. Vegetable Oil
1 Onion finely chopped
4 Scallions or Green Onions finely chopped
1 clove Garlic minced
4 medium Tomatoes peeled, seeded and chopped
2 Tbsps. Chiles diced
1/2 cup chopped Cilantro leaves
1/2 cup Water
Salt and Pepper to taste
4 oz. Butter
1/2-3/4 cup All-Purpose Flour
1 quart Milk
8 oz. Monterey Jack Cheese shredded
4 oz. Sharp Cheddar Cheese shredded
You can substitute cheeses of the same consistency.

1. Heat oil in a large saucepan. Add onion, scallions and garlic. Cook until tender but not browned. Add tomatoes and cook about 15 minutes over medium heat. Stir in chiles and cilantro. Add water. Add salt and pepper to taste. Set aside from heat.
2. In another large saucepan, heat butter until melted; stir in flour until the mixture looks like applesauce. Sauté over medium heat about 3 minutes, stirring constantly. Do not let flour burn.
3. Add milk and cheeses, stirring until the cheese melts and the mixture thickens. Add the vegetable mixture to the cheese mixture and stir to blend.
4. Place in a fondue pot (or crock pot) over a medium flame. Serve with chips.

Pozole

Ingredients:

Pork shoulder or roast -- 1 1/2 to 2 pounds
Canned or fresh hominy, rinsed -- 2 to 3 cups
Garlic -- 3 to 5 cloves
Ground cumin -- 2 teaspoons
Salt -- 2 teaspoons

Water or stock -- 6 cups
Cabbage or iceberg lettuce, shredded
Onion, finely diced
Radishes, thinly sliced
Limes, cut into wedges
Avocado, diced
Cilantro, chopped
Oregano, dried
Chile piquín, ground

1. Add the pork, hominy, garlic, cumin, salt and stock or water to a large pot. Bring to a boil over medium-high heat, and then reduce heat to low and simmer for 1 1/2 to 2 hours, or until the meat is very tender.
2. Remove the pot from heat. Take the pork from pot and set aside to cool. When cool enough to handle, remove the meat from its bones and shred it with your hands.
3. Add the meat back to the pot and simmer for another 10 to 15 minutes. Adjust seasoning and serve with little bowls of your choice of garnishes so each dinner can garnish his or her own serving.

Pozole Rojo (Red Pozole): This variation is popular in Michoacán and Jalisco States. It is the same as the above recipe, but dried chiles are added. Remove the stems and seeds from 3 to 5 ancho or guajillo chiles. Mix them with a little of the hot liquid from the stewpot and soak for 20 to 30 minutes until soft. Puree in a blender and strain through a sieve into the stew for the last 30 to 45 minutes of cooking.

Shrimp Enchiladas Corona

Ingredients:

12 large shrimp
2 Corona Beers
4 Tablespoons of butter
1 Tablespoon of olive oil
6 Chiles de arbol (cayenne)
4 Tablespoons of chopped onion
4 Tablespoons of chopped enchalotes
1/4 Heavy cream
3 Tablespoons of Worcestershire sauce
1 Tablespoon of salt
1 Tablespoon of pepper

Clean the shrimp and marinate in half the beer with some of the salt and pepper for at least one hour.

Sauté the onion and enchalotes in butter and olive oil, until they are clear, add the shrimp and sauté until they turn pink. Add the Worcestershire, salt and pepper.

Cut the chilies in halves and add with the cream, heat and stir.

Take the shrimp out and set apart. Add the remaining beer to the salsa and reduce heat to simmer for 15 minutes. While it is simmering, relax and drink the other Corona. Place the sauce in a serving plate add the shrimp on top, adorn with the chilies.

If you cannot find enchalotes, omit from the recipe

Horchata de Arroz

Ingredients:

Rice -- 2 cups
Water -- 6 cups
Cinnamon -- 1/2 teaspoon
Sugar -- 1/3 cup
Vanilla -- 1 teaspoon

1. Soak the rice overnight in 3 cups of the water. Add the rice, soaking water and cinnamon to a blender and puree until smooth, 2-3 minutes.
2. Strain into a pitcher through a fine-meshed sieve or several layers of cheesecloth. There should be no grit or large particles in the liquid.
3. Stir in the remaining 3 cups water, sugar and vanilla. Adjust sugar to taste and serve well chilled.

Substitute 3 cups of milk for 3 cups of the water. Or use evaporated milk for a richer, creamier version.

MEXICAN FOOD DEFINITIONS

Ancho Chile (AHN-choh)
The dried version of the popular POBLANO chile. It is about 3–4 inches long and a dark, reddish brown. It is the sweetest of all the dried chile's with a slightly fruity flavor. Used in making sauces.

Arroz(AH-roz)
Rice, usually referring to the long-grain, white variety

Barbacoa (bar-bu-KO-uh)
Mexican 'pot roast' made from the cows head. Seasoned and baked with steam for hours until it is peel apart tender.

Bolillo(bo-EE-yo)
Mexican ROLLS, usually about 6 inches in length.

Borracho (bo-ROTCH-o)
Made with beer, usually referring to cooked PINTO beans, that areserved like a soup.

Bunuelos (bun-WAY-los)
Fried tortilla-like pastries that are a favorite during the holiday season. They are traditionally sprinkled with cinnamon sugar and served with a scoop of ice cream.

Burrito (burr-EE-toe)
A large (10») flour tortilla filled with any number of concoctions including beans, beef, and pork-then sealed by tucking the ends under. They can be eaten like this or topped with salsa, lettuce, tomato, cheese, or guacamole.

Carne (CAR-nay)
Spanish and Mexican for meat, CARNE refers specifically to beef

Carne Asada—charcoal grilled pork or beef

Carne Guisada (CAR-nay GEE-sah-dah)
Stewed meat made with beef, onions, bell peppers, garlic, salt, pepper, comino that is then served over white rice, or with Spanish rice and refried beans.

Ceviche—fish, shrimp, conch marinated with limon, vinegar, onions, tomatoes and cilantro.
Chuleta Yucateca—Pork chop marinated in red adobado then grilled and smothered with sautéed onions

Cilantro—the spice known in the USA as coriander

Cochinita Pibil—pork marinated in a sauce of achiote, natural orange juice and spices, wrapped in fresh banana leaves, and slowly steamed.

111

Chorizo (CHORE-ee-so)
Mexican Sausage, made with ground pork and spicy seasonings. In
Mexico, fresh pork is used

Flan (flan)
A dessert that closest resembles a caramel custard.

Flauta (FLOU-ta)
Translates literally to "flute". This is a corn tortilla, usually white or yellow, that
has been stuffed with beef, chicken, pork, or even beans-then rolled and pinned,
then deep-fried until crisp.

Frijole con Puerco—A delicious local dish consisting of soupy black beans cooked
with chunks of pork. It's served with chopped radish, avocado, onion and cilantro
as garnish and steamed rice.

Guacamole (WOK-uh-mole-ee)
Avocado mixture that is made from ripened avocado's and lemon or lime juice,
diced onion and tomato, cilantro. Guacamole is made by mixing by hand with a fork
until the consistency still has very small (1/8») chunks of avocado. Never use a food
processor for making guacamole!!

Horchata—a cold soft drink made of rice or barley, almonds, sugar, vanilla and water

Huevos (WAY-vose)
Eggs.

Huachinango—red snapper—usually served whole

Jalapeno (hall-a-PEN-yo)
A pepper that turns from green to red at maturity, these average about 2 inches in
length. The 'hot' comes from the seed and membrane.
Jamaica—(ha-MY-ka) a delicious soft drink made from brewed hibiscus petals.

Masa (MAH-sah)
The Spanish word for "dough", masa is the corn flour dough used in making
corn tortillas, tamales and gorditas. Dried corn is cooked in lime water, cooled, and
then ground into masa.

Mero—fresh grouper usually served filet style

Mojo de Ajo—fish, coch or shrimp served in butter and garlic sauce

Mole—chicken or turkey meat or enchiladas baked in a thick spicy brown sauce made of almonds, chocolate chipotle peppers and peanut oil

Pan Dulce (pon-DUEL-say)
    Pan Dulce are dome-shaped Mexican sweet rolls that are distinctive by the "shell" design on top. Most have a sugar topping with chocolate, lemon and vanilla being favorites

Platano Frito—tasty fried bananas

Pollo (PO-yo) Chicken.

Queso (k-SO)
    Cheese. In Mexico, goat's cheese is used for traditional dishes.

Queso "Gallo"—a Holland cheese, the same as Gouda, that has been imported to the Yucatan for so many years that it is now considered indigenous to the area

Queso Relleno—seasoned, ground pork/beef formed into a round "loaf", completely surrounded in softened
Queso Gallo and then wrapped in cheesecloth for cooking. Served in round slices covered in cream sauce.

Ranchero (ran-CHAIR-o)
    With tomatoes, bell peppers, garlic and onions as the backdrop, the word RANCHERO is used to describe either a salsa (cooked) or how something is cooked.

Salsa (SAL-sa)
    Sauce, refers generally to a tomato based condiment used to dip or to accent dishes.

Serrano Chile (seh-RAH-noh)
    A small (1 1/2 inches) fresh HOT pepper. As it matures, it will turn red, then yellow. A general rule with chile's is that the smaller they are in size, the more kick they have. The serrano chile is almost always used when making "pico de gallo"

Taco (tah-KOH)
    A Mexican or Tex-Mex sandwich eaten as an entree or snack. They are made with soft corn tortillas, fried corn tortillas folded over, or with hot, flour tortillas.

Tamales—chicken wrapped in a heavy dough and cooked in banana leaves

Tomatillo (TOM-a-tea-yo)

A small green Mexican fruit that is part of the tomato family. They are tough to the touch and are covered with a brown husk. Used mainly in making sauces, either fresh (fresca) or after simmering and then putting in a food processor with spices. This is the sauce used when the word VERDE (green) is used, i.e.: Enchiladas Verde.

Torta (TORE-tah)
Mexican "sub" sandwich that is made on a bolillo". (white or wheat roll)

Tortilla (tore-TEE-yu)
It is a round, thin "bread" made of either corn flour or wheat flour. Tortillas are cooked quickly on a hot COMAL and are eaten by themselves or can be used to wrap around anything imaginable and eaten as tacos.

Coconuts on the east side, don't miss it.

CHAPTER VI

SHOP–SHOP–SHOP

Tee shirts to diamonds, you can find it in
Cozumel

LET'S SHOP, SHOP, SHOP

Handicrafts, souvenirs, tee shirts, pottery, jewelry, liquor, clothing, it is all available in Cozumel. The best bargain in jewelry is the silver. Be sure to purchase in stores and check for the .925 mark to assure you are getting real sterling and not nickel silver. For gem stones and gold you can do as good or better at home. I have purchased gold here but only for some of the unique designs and not any super bargain on price. Black coral is an exception, but be sure to buy from a licensed dealer.

Good buys can be found on Yucatecan hammocks, leather goods, embroidered and lace clothing and table linens, silver jewelry, ceramics and decorative metalwork and carved wood. You will also find high-quality handicrafts from all over Mexico—but because of the cost of importation to the island, you may find slightly better buys on these on the Mainland

Designer clothing is not a bargain here, but there are a few local stores that have designs you may not find at home, mostly sized for smaller women. Everyday clothing and beach wear is available at good prices. I used to arrive with only an overnight bag for myself, dedicating the rest of my luggage to my charities, so I usually purchased what I needed while here.

For small souvenirs such as ash trays, cups and glasses try the Chedraui store, better prices than in the tourist areas. Liquor can also be a bargain in this store and other local liquor stores. Be sure to get a bottle of Rum Pope a local liqueur great in coffee.

Electronics are not cheap in Mexico, so be sure to bring your CD player, cameras and film. I found this out when I paid at least 4 times the value to replace my son's portable CD player.

A brief listing of some of my favorite shops is included in this book, but just because a shop is not listed, does not mean you should not shop there. If you find a favorite not listed, please let us know. Have fun bargaining where you can, but please remember these fine people have to make a living, so do not expect them to give their merchandise away. Bargaining is more likely in the smaller shops and where the prices are not clearly marked.

SHOPPING AREAS

PLAZA AND WATERFRONT AREA

The downtown and Main Square is a beautiful area with numerous shops selling Mexican and Mayan handicrafts and souvenirs. Jewelry shop after jewelry shop will be found here.

PUNTA LANGOSTA

You will find plenty of trinket shops in addition to some very upscale shops at this mall, located at the downtown cruise pier. There is often entertainment here when the cruise ships are in. Enjoy the Mexican music and dancing.

PUERTO MAYA MALL

A new shopping area with many of the same stores that are located downtown and a few new ones. A nice place to stroll around and shop. It is located at the Puerto Maya cruise pier.

FORUM SHOPS
Melgar and Calle 10 Norte

The Forum Shops mall provides an assortment of upscale shops where you can save on jewelry, cigars, gifts, fine carpets, silver and more.

STORES

Alegria Infantil
Ave 5

They carry a unique selection of kid's toys and games.

ArtePaz
Behind the Museum on Calle 6 between the waterfront and Ave 5

Wholesaler of inexpensive beaded jewelry and enamel rings. You can bargain with the owner and get some really good deals.

Bien Raices
Melgar & Calle 8

All kinds of interesting, handcrafted objects, and you can bargain. Lots of things not found in other shops.

Bugamillias
Ave 10 between Salas and Calle 1

Specializing in handmade lace and embroidered and woven table linens and clothing. Beautiful clothing and linens of high quality

Café Optima de Chiapas
Calle 2 between Ave 5 & 10

They carry rich, freshly ground Mexican coffee from the Chiapas region. There is a good selection of beans and roasts.

Cariloha
Melgar between Calle 2 & Juarez

Cariloha is one of Cozumel's newest and most unique boutiques. What is not apparent when you first see the store is the fact that every item of clothing in the store is actually made with Bamboo!
Their clothing is super comfortable, odorless, keeps you cooler then cotton and has many other properties that make this line of goods truly island cool.

Casa Bella
Calle 3 between Avenida 5 and 10.

Moderately-priced and beautiful decorative items including silver trays, pottery, lamps and more are the buys you will find here.

Chedraui
Melgar between Calle 15 & 17gar

This is a Wal-Mart type store .It is bigger than the San Francisco store, and has slightly better prices. It's a good place to stock up at the beginning of your stay.

They take credit cards! It is great for food, clothing and cheap souvenirs. A good place to use your U.S dollars as the exchange rate is always good.

Covi Liquors
Ave 30 and Calle 2

This is one of the best places to buy your tequila, rum, kaluha, etc. This is where many of the locals shop. It is far away from the tourist shops in town so the prices are WAY lower. For example, the prices for my favorite tequilas are literally half what they cost at Cinco Soles

Crafts Market
Main Plaza

This is actually now Plaza del Sol. It is a large building with an assortment of shops. Be sure to go inside as there are more shops hiding inside..

Dichbe´h Tequila
2nd floor at Punta Langosta Mall

This is the best tequila I have ever tasted, It is not available in the USA. It comes in many flavors besides the regular. It is expensive but well worth it and he always gives you an extra gift of some sort, like another small bottle.

El Sombrero
Ave. Rafael Melgar 29

Stocks leather clothing and accessories. Good prices if you bargain, and it smells so good in there.

Funky Bazaar
Calle 15 (Xel Ha) between Ave 20 & 25

It features reasonably-priced, funky clothes, furniture, art and gifts. They also carry Humane Society t-shirts and pet accessories. Most of the clothing is gently used and donated. You can find some real treasures here.

Galleria Azul
Ave 10 between Salas and Calle 1

Original art of many talented Mexican artists can be found here. There is an ever changing assortment of paintings, sculpture, and more.

Galleria Alexander
Av. 5 # 141
Galleria Alexander carries ceramics and paper Mache works created by the Mexican artist Alexander Flores.

Hammock Shop
Ave 5 across the street from Zermatt's Bakery

Excellent buys from this Spanish man, but it helps if you speak some Spanish. He makes them himself

Havana Club Cigar Bar
Melgar and Calle 8.

This is your best place for variety, quality and price on individual cigars as well as boxes

House of Jeans
Calle 11 & Ave 15
Next to Oxxo

My daughter should have stock in this store. She goes crazy over the stylish jeans and great prices. They also carry many beautiful and unique tops to wear with those jeans.

Huaracheria Margarita
Ave 30 and Calle 3

This is a couple of stands on the corner displaying a wide assortment of sandals. They are handcrafted in some of the small villages of Mexico. You cannot find anything comparable in the USA and certainly not at these prices.

Instrumentales Musicales
Juarez and Ave 20

Musical instruments from all over Mexico are what you will find in this interesting little place. If you are a musician this needs to be on your list of things to see. There many things for sale and there are antique instruments on display.

Kite Cozumel
987 103 6711 (Local Cell)
Country Club Estates
Gear for kite surfing and other watersports from top instructor, Raul del Lille.
Authorized distributor for Slingshot, Raul has the very latest new equipment as well
as used gear for sale.

Kokorush
987- 120- 1317
1. Ave 30 between Juarez and 1 across from the gas station
2. Juarez between 10 and 15
3. Mega Super Store complex

Custom made perfume and knock off designer fragrances are sold here. Nice supply
of oils and they prepare several different strengths.

La Concha
5 Ave one half block from the Plaza.

You will find a wide assortment of gifts, folk art and weavings here.

Los Cinco Soles
Melgar & Calle 8
www.loscincosoles.com

Los Cinco Soles is a large store with crafts from all over Mexico, nice jewelry,
boutique section in the rear, and a 50% discount area. It is the most visited store by
tourists. If you only have time for one store, this would be the one. Prices are set
and no bargaining. Prices are fair and close to what you will get bargaining for the
same merchandise on the streets. **Los Cinco Soles is happy to offer the readers
of "Cozumel the Complete Guide II" a 10% discount on their purchase when
accompanied by the coupon in this book.**

Mayan Feather
Av. 5 and Calle 2

Mayan Feather has original paintings on feathers from birds of the area. Prices are
reasonable and many of the pictures are quite beautiful.

Melody
Juarez between Melgar & Ave 5
Calle 1 between Melgar & Ave 5h Plaza
There are the two locations right off the main plaza. Follow one of the two streets or walkways on either side of the clock. They carry a great assortment of women's and girls' clothing. The prices are low and there are always several sale racks in the front of each store.

MI CASA
Melgar 2 blocks north of Mall

This is the sister store to Cinco Soles, but I like it so much more. They carry beautiful Mexican dinnerware sets, Catrina figures, and so much more. They have a smaller inventory but everything is first class here.

Miguelon y Hijos
Calle 5 and Ave 15

This artist specializes in finely carved shell work that is very cameo like in style. His work is often on display at the museum.

Miro
Ave Rafael Melgar, near the ferry pier

Mexican resort wear with the latest designs and styles. Reasonable prices.

Milano Clothing Store
Calle 1 between Ave 15 & 10

Did you lose your luggage or forget to pack shorts? This is one of two good places to take care of the problem. Milano carries men/women/children's fashions at affordable prices. A very large selection of casual wear, lingerie and necessities is available along with racks of sale items as well. They have a wide selection and low prices.

Muebles de la Santa Cruz
Avenida 15 between Calle 2 and Juárez.

Furniture and accessories in the wrought iron and carved wood rustic style. there are lots of small things to choose including talevera, wood and wrought iron lamps, picture frames, etc. Prices are very reasonable and well below what you would pay in the states.

Na Balam
Ave 5 # 14

Specializes in Mayan artifact reproductions, textiles and fine jewelry.

Pama
Av. Rafael E. Melgar front corner of Plaza
987-872-0090

Pama is near the ferry pier, carries imported jewelry, perfumes, and glassware. They carry a full line of Pandora charms, beads, and bracelets. Their prices for perfume are very good.

Pepe the Puppet Man
Wandering the streets and Plaza

These puppets are not the same that you find in the stores. They arehome made by his wife and last forever. I have been buying them forfamily and friends for many years. Be sure to tell Pepe I sent you!

Pipo Liquors
Ave 30 and Calle 6

This is another good place to buy your tequila, rum, kaluha, etc. The prices are similar to COVI (check both places for your favorite items). Pipo has many brands that COVI doesn't carry.

Poco Loco
Av. Benito Juarez 2-A

Sells casual wear and beach bags. They have some nice resort wear. They Also have a large assortment of beach bags.

Puro Mar Surf-Kite-Bikini
www.cozumelkiteboarding.com/eng/shop.asp
Corner of 5 th Ave and Calle 3

Kite Board supplies, beach clothes, and the sexiest bikinis this side of Brazil. My daughter and niece buy at least 1 or 2 every time they visit.
They also carry some cute sandals. **Purchase a Kiteboard from Puro Mar Surf-Kite-Bikini Shop and get a free lesson with coupon.**

Rogers Boots
Corner of Rosado Salas & Melgar

You will find a large assortment of western boots and belts here along with other leather goods. Beware the designer purses, they are knock offs but you can get great deals by bargaining here.

Sam's Club
Calle 11 and Ave 75th area

Sam's Club, need I say more? The new store recently opened in July 2011. It is pretty much like any other Sam's Club. It is a good place to Shop if you have a large crowd.

Silver & Black Coral
20th Ave. between Juarez & Calle 2

I do not know the name of this store but it is owned and operated by Luis Calaca. This man has worked black coral all his life in Cozumel and his house/workshop is the place to shop He has a lot of silver jewelry for sale at good prices and the shop is a great place for earring and bracelet purchases. He has made several unique pieces as gifts for my family and has also done some silver repair for me. He furnishes certificates for his coral pieces, which are legal for export/import.

Spray Paint Artists
Front of the Plaza

These guys are talented and fun to watch. It is amazing to see what they can do. It is an inexpensive way to take home some memories. Bring some blank license plates and have them paint something unique.

The Talevera Store
Calle 1 between Ave 20 and 25

A large selection of hand-painted Mexican pottery and a lot of really beautiful authentically hand-painted Talevera style pottery. Prices are a lot better than you'll see for similar items in the gift shops, and far less than some of the similar items I have seen in the import stores in the states.

Talavera
Av. 5 # 349

Not the same as above, this is a more sophisticated store with some higher prices. Talavera carries beautiful ceramics from all over Mexico including tiles from the Yucatan, masks from Guerrero, brightly painted wooden animals from Oaxaca, and carved chests from Guadalajara.

Tanya Moss Design Jewelry
Punta Langosta, Ave Melgar

Jewelry with imaginative and innovative design that blends rich Mexican artistic heritage with the sophistication and versatility of Tanya Moss' own design ideas.

Unicornio
Av. 5 # 1
Just off the Plaza on the pedestrian walkway

Unicornio specializes in Mexican folk art, including ceramic notions and etched wooden trays, but you'll have to sift through a lot of souvenir junk to find the good-quality items.

Viva Mexico
Melgar & Salas

This is a large store on the waterfront with a good selection of both the usual Souvenirs, as well as some nicer pewter and ceramic pieces. They also have beautiful crafts from the Oaxaca area of Mexico. Staff are dressed in traditional attire and perform scheduled folk dances.

CHAPTER VII

DIVING

MAGICAL, MYSTICAL COZUMEL

DIVE COZUMEL

For many, the definition of Cozumel is diving. Ever since Jacques Cousteau discovered the diving on the reefs of Cozumel in 1961 divers have flocked to this Caribbean Island paradise. Because diving in Cozumel is drift diving (exactly what it sounds like), little energy is spent on swimming and bottom times are much longer. Visibility in the crystal blue waters is usually 100 ft. or more, sometimes reaching 200 feet.

The marine life here is awesome, bright, and beautiful. Colorful fish and coral, huge lobster, crab and Manta Rays. Giant sea turtles, and if you are lucky, you may see some dolphins, sharks, and even some seahorses. Dive at night and it becomes a magical mystical world of sea life.

If you have never dived before, most dive operations offer the resort course, which will teach you basics and allow you your first dive. This gives you a chance to sample the sport and make a decision to continue or not. There are over 45 dive operations on the island, I strongly advise that before you choose one that you log on to one of the Cozumel or Scuba discussion boards and ask questions. Divers are quick to share their satisfaction or disappointments about their dive experiences.

I have listed what I believe is most or all of the dive operations on the island, and a description of most of the dive sites. If for any reason I have missed an operator, I apologize and it is not to reflect badly on that operator, just inquire about him on the discussion boards.

A note about shore diving. Shore diving is available on the island, not as great as the diving available by boat, but still fun and interesting. Tanks are available at $6–$8 U.S.. Dive the old plane wreck in front of the La Ceiba, it has some nice marine life, and makes a neat night dive.

HAPPY DIVING, AND PLEASE DO NOT TOUCH THE CORAL.

DIVE OPERATIONS

ALDORA DIVERS
frontdesk@aldora.com
WWW.ALDORA.COM
011-52-987-872-4048
210-569-1203/1204
Calle 5 #37
Call or email for rates

AQUA SAFARI
WWW.AQUASAFARI.COM
011-52-987-872-0101
Av. Rafael Melgar #429

2 Tank large boat $70 additional dive $15
1 tank afternoon $35
2tank fast boat $75
Night dive $45
Snorkeler $25
Equipment rental and instruction available

AQUATIC SPORTS
www.scubacozumel.com
Scubacoz@scubacozumel.com
011-52-987-872-0640

2 tanks $75
Email for other rates. Instruction and rentals available

BLUE ANGEL
www.blueangel-scuba.com
blueangel@cozumel.com.mx
1-866-266-5639
contact for prices
Instruction and rentals available.

BLUE BUBBLE
www.bluebubble.com
Info@bluebubble.com

011- 52-987/872-4240
1tank $48
2 tank $70

Call for group and multi day packages.
BLUE NOTE SCUBA DIVING
www.bluenotescuba.com
011- 52-987-872-0312

2 tank $86
Night dive $60

Call for packages

BLUE XT SEA DIVING
Info@bluextseadiving.com
www.bluextseadiving.com
011-52-987-869-8574
800-281-0134

2 tank $75-79
3 tank $120
Night dive $50 Instruction available

Christi gets excellent reviews and divers return to her over and over. She is well known for going out of her way to help fellow divers, even when they are not her customers. Prices can vary depending on customized packages. Contact Christi today so she can customize your dive vacation. Packages with lodging available.

BUENA VENTURA
 www.gocozumel.com/ventura   contact for rates and information
Ventura@gocozumel.com
011-52-987-872-6014

CABALLITO DEL CARIBE
www.seahorsecozumel.com
Caballitocozumel@prodigy.net.mx
011-52-987-872-1449

1tank $50
2 tank $70
Night dive $50
Multi day available. Instruction and gear rental available

CARIBBEAN DIVERS
www.cozumel-diving.net/caribbean_divers/
011-52-987-872-1080

Caribbean Divers is one of the oldest and most prestigious dive operators in Cozumel. Owned and operated by Cesar Zepeda and his famous crew. Operating since 1977

Call or email for rates

CAREYCITOS ADVANCED DIVING
www.advanceddivers.com
011-52-987-872-0111

Starting January 2011 Careyitos advanced divers teams up with the Moon Diver, a 90foot live aboard vessel, with 8 double/triple occupancy staterooms complete with bathroom and A/C.

Contact for pricing. Gear and instruction available

COZUMEL SPORTS
www.cozumelsports.com
info@cozumelsports.com
011- 52-987- 872-0000

2 tank $75
1tank $50
Night dive $50

DEEP EXPOSURE
www.deepexposuredivecenter.com
866- 670- 2736
011- 52-(987- 872 3621

1 tank	$52
2 tank	$87
Night dive	$62

DEL MAR AQUATICS
Reservations@delmaraquatics.net
www.delmaraquatics.net
011-52-987-872-5949

Call for rates. Instruction and gear rental available.

DIMI SCUBA
www.dimiscubatours.com
Info@dimiscubatours.com
011-52-987-872-2915

Contact for rates. Instruction and gear rental available.

DIVE PALANCAR
www.divepalancar.com
reservations@divepalancar.com
011-52-987 872- 9730 EXT. 6264

Contact for rates. Instruction and gear rental available.

DIVE PARADISE
Questions@diveparadise.com
www.diveparadise.com
011-52- 872-1007
011-52-869-0503

1 tank $33
2 tank $65-75
Instruction and gear rental available.

DIVE WITH MARTIN
www.cozumel-diving.net/martin
divewithmartin@gmail.com

1 TANK $60
2 TANK $80
3 TANK $100

Contact for rates./multi day

DIVING ADVENTURES COZUMEL
www.divingadventures.net
dive@divingadventures.net
011-52-987-872-3009

Contact for rates. Instruction and gear rental available.

DRESSEL DIVERS
www.dresseldivers.com
Sales@dresseldivers.com

Contact for rates. Instruction and gear rental available.

EAGLE RAY
www.eagleraydivers.com
011-52-987-872-5735
866-465-1616
Chellie@eagleraydivers.com

2 tank $70
3 tank $88
Night dive $45

ECO DIVERS
www.cozumel-diving.net/ecodivers
ecodivers@cozumel-diving.net
800-746-2709

2 tank $72
Twilight 2tank $82
Night dive $57

Instruction and gear rental available.

EMERALD DOLPHIN
www.cozumel-diving.net/edds
reservations@we-b-divin-cozumel.com
800-935-5604
AKA we-b-divin
Contact for rates.Instruction and gear rental available.

LUIS CABANAS

lusis@cozumel.com.mx

011-52-987-872-6745

Specialized in custom advanced dive trips, cave and cenote diving.
Contact for rates. Instruction and gear rental available.

MESTIZO DIVERS

www.mestizodivers.com

011 521 987 103 7120

2 tank $80   call for other rates

PAPA HOGS

www.papahogs.com

Scubadiving@PapaHogs.com

011-52-987-872-1651

2 tank $65
Night dive $45
Instruction and gear rental available.

Mike and Margaret have been here for a long time and have a large following. Personally
I recommend them because my granddaughter chooses to dive with them.

SAND DOLLAR SPORTS

www.sanddollarsports.com

sds@sanddollarsports.com

888 663 3140

Contact for rates. Instruction and gear rental available.

SCUBA DU DIVE

www.scubadu.com

INFO@SCUBADU.COM

011- 52 -987- 872-9500 X6855

310- 684-5556

2 Tank Morning $88
2 Tank Afternoon $88 Min. 4 divers

2 Tank Special Trip $105 Min. 4 divers
2 Tank Twilight & Night Dive $88 Min. 4 divers
1 Tank to Paradise Reef $55 Min. 4 divers
1 Tank Night Dive $55 Min. 4 divers

SCUBA TONY
Info@scubatony.com
WWW.SCUBATONY.COM
011-52- 987 869-8268
626- 593-7122

2 Tank $85
Night Dive $55

SCUBA WITH ALLISON
www.scubawithalison
alison@scubawithalison.com
cell 011-52-1-987-878-5071
011-52-987-989-6269
This gal provides a more personal approach to diving and instruction.

Contact for rates. Instruction and gear rental available.

SEA URCHIN DIVE
Diving@seaurchindive.com
www.seaurchindive.com
011-52-987-878-4888
2 tank $64
2 tank twilight $65
Night dive $45

Contact for multi day rates. Instruction and gear rental available.

Formerly owned and operated by Isidro, many doubted Jorge would be able to carry on the high standards expected by Isidro's customers. The reviews are in and Jorge has passed with flying colors.

WILDCAT DIVERS
www.amproductions.com/wildcat.html
Wildcatcozumel@hotmail.com

011-52-987-872-1028
Contact for rates. Instruction and gear rental available

YUCATECH EXPEDITIONS
www.yucatech.net
german@germanyanez.com
011-52-987 113 7044

Great operation for cave, technical and rebreather diving in Mexico. Training instructors, guides, and divers at all levels of recreational and technical diving.

Contact for pricing and more information

COZUMEL DIVE SITES

Airplane Wreck (Shore) Skill Level: Novice
Location: In front of la Ceiba Hotel.
Conditions: Shallow and sheltered
Minimum depth: 33 ft. /10 m
Maximum depth: 40 ft. /12 m

Hurricane Roxanne hit in 1995 the small plane is now broken up and scattered over the area, setting about 210ft/65m from the pier. The remains of the aircraft are now home to a large assortment of grunts and snapper. On the shore side of the wreck the sea bed rises rapidly to 17ft/5m and the numerous small coral heads have large numbers of Christmas tree worms and the split-crown feather duster on them. Hermit crabs, numerous shrimps and several species of blenny are among the sea fans and plumes.

Balones of Chankanaab
Depth: Shallow Dive: 60 to 70 feet
Skill level: Novice
A series of balloon—shaped coral heads. Lots of marine life, lobster and crab. Barge Wreck (Shore, Boat) Skill Level: Intermediate
Location: Opposite the Vista Del Mar Hotel.
Conditions: Currents to be expected, windy and surface chop between November and April.
Minimum depth: 60ft
Maximum depth: 70 ft.

A large series of balloon-shaped coral heads teaming with all sorts of marine critters. The limestone shoreline of this area is very porous and often fresh water runoff will diminish visibility especially after heavy rains. Still worth diving regularly due to abundance of crab and lobster. Excellent night dive.

Barge Wreck (Shore, Boat) Skill Level: Intermediate
Location: Opposite the Vista Del Mar Hotel.
Conditions: Currents to be expected, windy and surface chop between November and April.
Minimum depth: 30 ft. /9 m
Maximum depth: 40ft/12m

The barge was sunk in 1976 and is now abundant with sea life. There are many different corals and all sea life. The barge is 100ft., 30 m. long by 30 ft., 9m. Wide and 10ft., 3m. Height and sits upright on the bottom. There are two safe access points to the interior. The barge is a great night dive and photographers, should not miss it. There are large green moray eels and lots of black, Nassau.

Barracuda Wall (Boat) Skill Level: Advanced
Location: South of Punta Molas Lighthouse, to the Northwest of the island.
Conditions: Strong currents expected; windy with Surface chop.
Minimum depth: 45 ft. /14m
Maximum depth: beyond 100ft/30m
The most Northerly reef reached by any Cozumel dive operator, is seldom visited. Prior arrangements must be made through the harbor master. Due to the severity of the currents in the area, the number of divers per boat that can be carried on one trip is limited to six and all must be experienced open water drift divers, This is a flat strip reef with sand around, sloping into the depths. The attraction is the above-average chance to see large pelagic, such as barracuda, jacks, rays and sharks. Very large barrel sponges, rope sponges and elephant's ear sponge can all be found here.

Barracuda Reef (Boat) Skill Level: Advanced
Location: South of Punta Molas lighthouse, to the northwest of the island.
Conditions: A windy site with surface chop and strong currents.
Minimum depth: 69 ft. /21 m
Maximum depth: Beyond 100ft/30 m
This site is visited but prior arrangements must be made through the harbor master. There are severe currents in this area, so the number of divers per boat is limited to six and all must be experienced open-water drift divers. This is a flat strip reef sand around, sloping into the depths. The attraction is the above-average chance to

see large pelagic, such as barracuda, jacks, rays and sharks. The great barracuda (Sphyraena barracuda) is the most common species sighted. Diving here can be exhilarating, but hard work.

C-53 Wreck Xicotencatl
Depth: 80'
Skill level: Novice to Intermediate

Marked by a highly visible buoy, the ship is 184 feet long & 33 feet wide, and has 4 decks. The sinking by the Mexican Navy & wreck experts was a perfect job as it rests almost perfectly upright & flat with the bow facing SSE & stern NNW. The superstructure starts at 26', the main deck at 54' & the bottom, which is secured to prevent movement in storms, is at 78'. The craft is intact as sunk with the exception of one rudder which is now about 25' to the stern.

Cedral Wall (Boat)
Depth: Deep Dive: 50 to 90 feet
Skill level: Intermediate

Expect a good ride on the usually strong currents. Kind of flat but it is full of color and marine life.

Chankanaab Caves (shore)
Depth: 35 feet max
Skill level: Novice

This is an interesting dive at the south end of Chankanaab Park. Excellent beach dive that can be reached either from Chankanaab Park itself or by entering south of the park towards Corona beach where there is no park entrance fee. Cold fresh water flows out of limestone caves called cenotes. Large Tarpon can be found swimming around in the entrance to the caves. Stay in the ambient light and do not venture far back. Interesting mix of cold fresh water on the top layer with the warm salt water below.

Columbia Reef (Boat)
Depth: Deep Dive: 60 to 90 feet
Skill level: Intermediate
Impressive drop off at 60 to 80 feet. Deep diving at its finest, at least as spectacular as any part of the Palancar. A series of gigantic coral pinnacles, most over 90 feet, marked with caves, tunnels and caverns. Large marine life such as eagle rays, turtles and large barracuda often seen.

Columbia Shallow (Boat)
Depth: Shallow Dive: 15 to 35 feet max
Skill level: Novice
Maximum bottom time. This never ending sea garden is a favorite 2nd dive for maximum bottom time.

El Islote (Boat) Skill Level: Intermediate
Location: Close to Punta Celarain lighthouse traveling north toward the

Maya ruins at Tumba del Caracol
Conditions: An exposed location with unpredictable currents. This site is only accessible during the calmer months between May and September.
Minimum depth: 10 ft. /3 m
Maximum depth: 30 ft. /9 m

This single large coral Island is situated on flat sand and is a natural haven for all kinds of sea life. The shallower areas inshore split up into less distinct spur and groove reef formations. An interesting dive site, but there is always surge present. Good for parrotfish.

La Villa Blanca Drop-Off (Shore, Boat)
Location: Opposite La Villa Blanca Hotel.
Conditions: Strong currents to be expected, and surface can be choppy and windy.
Minimum depth: 69 ft. /21 m
Maximum depth: Beyond 100 ft. /30 m

This is a wall dive, but unlike the walls to the southwest of the island, which are vertical, it slopes steeply. This dive is one for experienced divers only. The currents can be quite strong and you do not get much chance to see the marine life unless it is swimming next you. If you dive from shore, make certain before you start that the current is running from the south to the north, this will make for an easier exit if you get swept away. A lot of work and questionable as to if it is worth the trouble.

La Ceiba Reef Preserve (Shore, Boat)
Location: Directly out from la Ceiba Hotel.
Conditions: Shallow, sheltered, good for beginners, photographers and snorkelers.
Minimum depth: 20 ft. /6 m
Maximum depth: 40 ft. /12 m
Skill Level: Novice

This is a ridge of coral and patch reef interspersed with sandy areas. There are star corals, brains corals, pillar corals and gorgonian sea fans. Beware of the Fire coral it HURTS. This dive is good for fish, sergeant majors and the yellowtail damselfish.

La Francesa Reef (Boat)
Location: Inner strip reef between Palancar and Santa Rosa reef.
Conditions: Moderate current and in most of this location, running from south to north.
Minimum depth: 40 ft. /12 m
Maximum depth: Beyond 66 ft. /20 m
Skill Level: Novice-Intermediate

This mostly unbroken strip and patch reef is the outer edge of la Francesa. It Bottoms out at 66 ft. /20 m but the coral rubble and sand slope continues down to the outer reef edge and drop-off. The inside of the reef has a gradual slope of sand running down to the reef and, in some cases, sand chutes completely dissect the reef. Southern stingrays, peacock flounders and various mollusks are to be found on the sand. There are nice corals and a large supply of fish and invertebrates.

Little Caves (Boat)
Depth: Deep Dive: 50 to 70 feet
Skill level: Novice

Great dive with winding, colorful canyons, deep ravines and narrow crevices. Lots of passageways, tunnels and caves. Great dive at 50–70 ft.

Maracaibo Reef (Boat)
Location: Close to Punta Celarain lighthouse and south from Colombia reef.

Conditions: An exposed location with unpredictable currents. Only the most experienced of divers should consider diving this location.
Minimum depth: 60 ft. /18 m
Maximum depth: Beyond 100 ft. /33 m
Skill Level: ADVANCED ONLY

This very deep reef and steeply inclined wall are subject to unpredictable currents. When descending through open water to reach the descending terraces you must move swiftly and keep close in to the reef or you may be swept away from your planned position on the reef. You can look in wonder at the complexity of the old coral limestone structures, caverns, caves and swim throughs. Only the most advanced divers should dive here and only with supervision of an experienced local dive master carrying a signal marker buoy and a very experienced boat captain.

Paradise Reef (Boat, Shore with a long swim)
Depth: Shallow Dive: 40 to 50 feet
Skill level: Novice

A series of three separate reefs running parallel to shore approximately 200 yards out. This is the only reef accessible to beach divers. All three sections have abundant marine life including the reclusive Splendid Toad Fish, reputed to live only in Cozumel. Most popular spot for night dives.

Punta Tunich Drop-Off (Boat)
Location: Opposite Punta Tunich, several hundred yards or meters further out than Yucab, but running parallel with the reef.
Conditions: Generally strong current and choppy surface conditions.
Minimum depth: 50 ft. /15 m
Maximum depth: Beyond 100 ft. /30 m
Skill Level: Intermediate

The Northern end of this reef is the most interesting, but it is better to approach it when there is south-to-north current running. The wall at this end is near vertical, with numerous caves and crevices, which bisect the reef, running from the crest at around 66ft/, 20m down to much deeper water. Squirrelfish and pairs of angelfish can be approached fairly easily. A number of very large green moray eels can be seen along this reef.

Paso del Cedral Reef (Boat)
Location: Opposite to Punta Cedral to the inside of and running parallel to Santa Rosa reef.
Conditions: A moderate current runs from south to north. Can be windy on the dive boat.
Minimum depth: 33 ft. /10 m
Maximum depth: 60 ft. /18 m
Skill Level (novice)

Good photography dive with lots of opportunities to photograph schooling fish. There are large Schools of grunt and snapper, particularly the blue striped grunt and the schoolmaster. The Corals are fairly short, as you would imagine on this exposed strip reef, but where the reef is cut by sand chutes there are some very interesting small coral, such as disk coral and cactus coral. The southern stingray feeds in the sandy areas to the inside of the reef. Among the many mollusks is the occasional the queen conch, which is becoming scarce.

Paso del Cedral Wall (Boat)
Location: The next large reef system to the south and west of Paso del Cedral Reef.
Conditions: Unpredictable strong currents are to be expected. Minimum depth: 40 ft. /12 m
Maximum depth: Beyond 100 ft. /30 m Skill Level: Intermediate

This site is similar to Santa Rosa Wall. It is less convoluted with fewer huge coral buttresses, but still very spectacular. Large grouper hang off the edge and numerous parrotfish are all over the area. Large encrusting and tube sponges, and many species of gorgonian fan corals to see.

Palancar Shallows (Boat)
Location: About 2 km (1 mile) offshore, inside and parallel to the Palancar Drop-off and to the north.
Conditions: Slight-to-moderate current. Exposed on the surface.
Minimum depth: 17 ft. /5 m
Maximum depth: 69 ft. /21 m
Skill Level: Novice

This is a very interesting reef offering a wealth of diving experiences without the need to travel far. It rises to about 60 ft. /18 m. The strip reef is more than 66 ft. /20 m wide in much of the area and is cut and dissected by many fissures and caves. There may be current flowing over the reef, but there are so many sheltered areas and shallow water that it never causes problems Large stove-pipe sponges fan out from the reef and there are black coral in the deeper areas. Bright yellow tube sponges may be associated with juveniles of the yellow head wrasse and other fish hide in the deep tubes for protection at night. Butterfly fish, angelfish, parrot fish and damsel fish can always be seen. To the south, before Palancar Caves the reef drops much lower and becomes less defined. Do not miss this dive!

Palancar Garden (Boat)
Location: About 2 km (1 mile) offshore, inside and parallel to the Palancar Drop-off and to the north.
Conditions: Slight-to-moderate current. Exposed on the surface.
Minimum depth: 17 ft. /5 m
Maximum depth: 69 ft. /21 m
Skill Level Novice   See description for Palancar Shallows.

Palancar Horseshoe (Boat)
Location: South of Palancar shallows, but before Palancar Caves is reached.
Conditions: Windy and exposed on the surface, There can be strong current, but it is sheltered in the horseshoe.
Minimum depth: 30 ft. /9 m
Maximum depth: Beyond 100 ft. /30 m
Skill Level: Intermediate

This is a natural amphitheater shaped like a giant horseshoe in a stretch in Palancar reef. There is plenty for any diver to enjoy in just one spot. The dive is best in the deeper section, which is deeply convoluted. Large gorgonian sea fans stretch out into the current and there is an array of fish, corals and invertebrates. The caves always attract divers, but you have to be very careful with controlling buoyancy so that you do not knock into the minute coral organisms that inhabit these shady areas. Remember to take a light with you to see the true colors of the animals and corals

Palancar Caves (Boat)
Location: South of The Horseshoe.
Conditions: There is generally a current, but you will scarcely feel the effect of it until you emerge through the caves on to the outer wall of the reef.
Minimum depth: 20 ft. /6 m
Maximum depth: Beyond 100 ft. /30 m   Skill Level: Intermediate

Although this is classified as a deep dive, the shallowest part of the reef comes to within 20 ft. /6 m of the surface. The reef slopes outward to the reef edge and deeply convoluted lip. Here, the corals seem to take on a life of their own as they form spires and buttresses, caves, gullies and canyons. Deep fissures run under the corals and sand slopes plummet into the depths. Large sheet corals jut out from the reef, creating interesting overhangs, which squirrel fish and bigeye seek during the day. There are countless caves and canyons along this stretch of reef and you will never be able to see all of them even after several dives. Schooling fish, such as grunts and snapper, constantly appear, and if you take your time as you exit the caves on the outer edge of the reef, you may glimpse a green turtle or a spotted eagle ray cruising past the wall

Palancar Deep (Boat)
Location: The outer of the reef wall south of the Horseshoe and Palancar caves.
Conditions: Exposed on the topside, and current is to be expected. Divers may experience difficulty climbing into the dive boat due to the sea swell.
Minimum depth: 40 ft. /12 m
Maximum depth: Beyond 100 ft. /30 m
Skill Level: Intermediate

This deeply incised wall is an absolute delight. There are so many different combinations of coral, you are never bored. Gorgonian sea fans on top of the reef and there is constant competition for space between the corals, sponges and algae. All are brightly colored and seem to have their own associated fish, crustaceans or invertebrates. Look out for a number of cleaning stations along this reef. Several different species host these locations, such as juvenile Spanish hogfish on the reef top, the cleaning goby among the coral head and the Pederson's cleaning shrimp among the tentacles of various species of anemone in the recesses.

Paso el Cedral (Oak Pass) (boat)
Depth: Shallow: 35 to 60 feet
Skill level: Intermediate

A series of many reefs marked with expansive low profile caverns at the beginning and lots of big fish. Less dived than most spots, but not to be missed.

Punta Sur Reef (Boat)
Location: South of Punta Sur at the southern entrance to Laguna Colombia.
Conditions: This site can be very exposed during extreme weather conditions and there is always current. Minimum depth: 80 ft. /24 m
Maximum depth: Beyond 130 ft. /40 m
Skill Level: Advanced

There is an inner strip reef, which rapidly falls away to what is becoming one of the most popular dive locations on the island.

Although the site can be visited only when weather permits, the sheer majesty of the deep wall, caves, caverns and fissures put the site at the top of most divers' lists. You enter the larger of the cave systems down a sand chute at 90ft/27 m where you enter a superb complex of coral tunnels and caverns, which are absolutely bursting with life. One of the larger caves, called the Devil's throat, opens up into an underwater room with four passageways, one of which leads to the Cathedral, a vast cavern with another three passageways, all interconnecting. The usual angelfish and butterfly fish can always be spotted swimming in pairs along the reef edge. The deeper coral walls have whip corals, which spiral out into the depths, and large black corals. There are also brightly colored small gorgonian sea fans, such as the deep-water fan, and sea whips, including the devil's sea whip, are very much evidence. This is an awesome dive, but bottom time is limited because of the extreme depth and the complex nature of the site.

San Francisco Reef (boat, shore)
Depth: Shallow: 35 to 50 feet
Skill level: Intermediate

Begins on the Southern end of Old San Francisco Beach. This half mile reef is broken into three sections, separate by about 60 yards of sand. This is Cozumel's shallowest wall dives and loaded with life between 35 and 50 feet.

San Juan Two (Boat)
Location: South of Punta Molas lighthouse, to the Northwest of the island.
Conditions: Strong currents always expected; windy with surface chop.
Minimum depth: 52 ft. /16 m

Maximum depth: Beyond 100ft/30 m
Skill level: Advanced

San Juan Two is a continuation of San Juan Reef. Severe currents flow through this area and the number of divers per boat is limited to six experienced open-water divers. This is a flat strip reef with sand around, sloping into the depths. This is the Northerly range of reef corals in this area of the Caribbean and the few varieties of coral that grow in this area are large. Large pelagic fish, such as eagle rays and sharks, are sometimes encountered around this site also.

San Juan Reef (Boat)
Location: South of Punta Molas lighthouse, on the same reef as San Juan Two.
Conditions: Strong currents always expected; and only for experienced divers.
Minimum depth: 69 ft. /21 m
Maximum depth: 80 ft. /25 m
Skill level: Advanced

Similar to San Juan Two, but the terrain is more uneven. Permission to dive must be granted by harbor master. Wire coral and purple sea fans are common, but the large pelagic are the attraction here; the gray reef shark (Carcharhinus perezi) is often seen. This dive is not for the faint-hearted. It is a long way to journey just for the chance of seeing big fish, and exploring it is hard work. There is a natural amphitheater called Pino's Bowl.

Santa Maria Reef (Boat)
Depth: Shallow: 40 to 60 feet
Skill level: Intermediate

This reef begins where San Francisco ends. A little less coral but large schools of angelfish.

Santa Rosa Wall (Boat)
Location: Next large reef system.
Conditions: Unpredictable strong currents are to be expected. There is always shelter however, when you reach the reef.
Minimum depth: 33 ft. /10 m
Maximum depth: Beyond 100 ft. /30 m
Skill Level: Intermediate

Easily be split into three separate dives. Its profile becomes larger and more convoluted the further North you travel. As in any exposed area, the Southernmost section is low-lying and scoured by currents. The middle section has some very large tunnels which completely cut through the reef crest, and the most northerly section has tunnels, caves, overhangs and under-hangs and some sections of wall becoming so steep they are near-vertical. On the steeper slopes there are numerous rope sponges. File clams can be seen in the recesses, their orange or white tentacles waving in the current. Many species of hermit crab can be found and there appear to be thousands of tiny gobies and blennies flitting in bursts over the corals and sponges. Barracuda and large specimens of the back grouper which shelter under the overhangs above the reef crest, can always be observed here. Stoplight parrot fish seem to blend into the multi-colored reef. Only when you use an underwater torch does true beauty of the reef reveal itself. One of the most distinctive of the small reef fish is the fairy basslet. The front half of its body is a brilliant violet-to-purple and its rear is a deep yellow/gold. These fish are instantly recognizable, but very hard to photograph because of their constant motion.

Torments Reef (Boat)
Location: South of Chankanaab Marine National Park and before Yucab reef, directly opposite Punta Tormentos.
Conditions: There can be very strong current.
Minimum depth: 30 ft. /9 m
Maximum depth: 69 ft. /21 m
Skill Level: Novice-Intermediate

An exposed, wide spread, broken-up patch reef system interspersed with wide, sandy channels.. It drops steeply to 69 ft. /21m on the outward side of the slope, where there is a secondary reef. The reef consists of around 60 separate coral heads covered in a wide variety of brain corals, sea fans and whip corals. Colorful sponges in the canyons and there are many invertebrates hiding in the rocky crevices. At the end of the dive, as the current takes you gently north, there is a huge underwater formation similar to a terrestrial sand dune. Although the current can occasionally be strong, the boat captains are experienced along this reef and will drift along with you in the current. Schools of Creole wrasse move over the reef crest, and Bermuda chub and yellowtail snapper are well used to being fed.

Virgin Wall (Boat)
Depth: Deep: 40 to 130 feet
Skill level: Expert

Heavy currents prevent dive masters from bringing in large groups of inexperienced divers. 2 to 4 different dives to experience it all.

Yucab (Boat)
Location: To the South of Punta Tormentos.
Conditions: There is usually current. The reef is scoured by sand movement and has many archways and overhangs.
Minimum depth: 40 ft. /12 m
Maximum depth: 69 ft. /21 m
Skill Level: Novice-Intermediate

Although all these reefs are essentially drift dives, Yucab also offers shelter from the current on the outer edges, where underwater photographers can be inspired by every color in the rainbow. The sand-scoured overhangs also offer refuge for lobsters, banded coral shrimps and the arrow crab. There are also large numbers of squirrel fish and angel and butterfly fish always swimming in pairs. Lots of parrot fish can be found around the live coral and you can hear their crunching on the coral.

Yucab Wall (Boat)

Location: Due west of Yucab.

Conditions: Current is to be expected, but the numerous large overhangs and tunnels across the reef offer plenty of protection for divers wanting to explore its recesses.

Minimum depth: 33 ft. /10 m

Maximum depth: Beyond 100 ft. /30 m

Skill level: all

This site is favored by a number of diving operations and it gets particularly busy along the outer reefs. Large coral buttresses jut out and form a convoluted, scalloped outer reef edge with numerous gullies and swim throughs. Like most of the outer reefs, Yucab Wall does not have many fish, but the fish that inhabit the site are large—such as black grouper. This is a particularly nice dive and its popularity is well deserved.

Marine Park Rules

Mexican government declare a National Marine park on July 19, 1996; covering area of more than 11 thousand hectares including the beaches and waters between Paradise Reef and Chiqueros point. The environmental, natural resource and fishing Secretariat SEMARNAP, administers the park.

The financing of the parks programs is shared by the federal government and the civil environmental groups; represented by COPRENAT, and the dive operators through ANOAAT.

Do your share to preserve the flora and fauna for future generations.

Corals are fragile.

Kicking, touching, dragging your gear causes damage, buoyancy control is your key to healthy coral.

Photographers in particular, take pictures without causing damage.

Marine organisms are protected by law.

Fishing, feeding the fauna and taking souvenirs is against the law.

Refrain from extracting or annoying the marine flora and fauna.

Help us prevent pollution.

Report fuel, oil, sewage and garbage spills to the National Park office.

Pressure your dive operator to instruct novice divers and divers without adequate buoyancy control, and to refuse service to destructive divers.

If you use gloves, do not grab the corals.

If you carry a knife, keep it in the sheath.

Use biodegradable sun block products.

CHAPTER VIII

FISHING IN

COZUMEL

Well before Cozumel became a diving Mecca, it was considered to be one of the top world class fishing destinations for sports fishing. You can bottom fish, sports and deep sea fish, or fly fish, whatever your heart's desire, there is an operator in Cozumel to give you what you want. Your choice of operators is diverse. You can go with the expensive top of the line fishing boats and pay top dollar, or you can go out with one of the less expensive operators, who has an older boat, but wonderful crews, and the equipment works the same, after all the fish don't know if that bait is hanging off a row boat or a yacht. Depending on the season you can expect to catch Sailfish, Blue and White Marlin (these are catch and release only), Wahoo, Grouper, Snapper, just to name a few.

The prime fishing season is March through October. Local fisherman fancy catching dorado (mahi-mahi), Wahoo, kingfish, sailfish, blue and white marlin and grouper (to name but a few). The crews supply the necessary fishing gear, lures, bait, beverages and snacks. You provide the energy.

During the high season (April through July) you can expect to catch Blue Marlin, White Marlin, Sailfish, Dolphin and Tuna. Year round, expect to catch Wahoo, Grouper, Barracuda, Mackerel, Amberjack and Snapper.

Sports fishing is primarily catch and release,. Pull that beauty in, take the picture and send him back to tease other fisherman. Grouper, snapper, Mahi Mahi, yummy, these guys are all keepers. Let the crew fillet them, share some with the crew and take the rest to your villa or a restaurant for cooking. It couldn't get it any fresher.

Tournaments

April

International Sport-fishing Tournament: This event brings together serious fishermen from all over the world to fish for mahi-mahi, tuna, blue marlin, white marlin, sailfish, Wahoo and red snapper. Each afternoon at 5pm the weighing begins. Be sure to be on the pier as each crew brings their catch to be qualified.

May

National Sport-fishing Tournament: This is an exciting weekend when all local and nationally registered boats compete for thousands of pesos in prizes including cars, boats, motorbikes and cash. You can catch the morning rally at the main ferry pier downtown where the beer is flowing and the water balloons are flying! Each afternoon at 5pm you can join the fishermen on the same pier to watch as each fish is weighed and scored.

CHARTER OPERATORS

3 HERMANOS
www.cozumelfishing.com
Scathed@prodigy.net.mx
011-52-987-872-6417
651-755-4897

ALBATROS CHARTER S
www.cozumel-fishing.net
Info@cozumel-fishing.net
011-52-987-872-7904
888-333-4643

½ day 1–6 people $420-450
¾ day 1–6 people $500-575
Full day 1–6 $575-650

FISHING COZUMEL
info@ fishingcozumel.net
www.fishingcozumel.net
877-260-7751
011-52-987-869-8560

Formerly known as Wahoo tours, this operation has grown from one boat to 28 available boats. They offer everything from economy to full blown luxury boats. My family has fished with the Wilson family for 15 years. We have never been disappointed. They also have fly fishing charters.
Rates $280-$1050

MARATHON
www.haciendasanmiguel.com/marathon.htm
Info@haciendasanmiguel.com

½ day $450 Jan–May 14 $500 April 15–May 30
 June–Dec
Full day $500 $550

OCEAN TOURS
www.cozumel-diving.net/oceantur
oceantours@usa.net
011-52-987-872-1379

½ day $440
Full day $600

SCUBA DU
www.scubadu.com/fishing.asp
scubadu@usa.net
011- 52-(987- 872-9500 X6855

½ day $393
Full day $523

SPEARFISHING COZUMEL
www.spearfishingtoday.com
011-52-1-987-876-0862

Leo has the original spearfishing adventure on Cozumel. Everything I have heard locally about him is good. He will instruct beginners, take families, and take the old pros. Call him for rates and information.

SPANISH FISH NAMES

AMBERJACK PEJE FUERTE
BONEFISH MACABI
BONITO BONITO
DOLPHIN/MAHI MAHI DORADO
GROUPER MERO
JACK JUREL
POMPANO PALOMETA
RED SNAPPER HUACHINANGO
SAILFISH PEZ VELA
SHARK TIBURON
SNAPPER PARGO

Brenda and Darlene on a beach front ride.

CHAPTER IX

BEACHES–TOURS

THINGS TO DO

You can't get bored here!

BEACHES, TOURS AND THINGS TO DO

If you don't dive or fish, not to worry my friend, there is so much else to do in Cozumel, you will not have time to get it all in. There are beaches to swim and snorkel at, or just relax, read a book, get a suntan, and let the waiters bring you a cold drink.

There is a wide assortment of tours and tour companies, sight-seeing and other activities. Spend a morning exploring the ruins of San Gervasio, take a horseback ride on the beach or thru the jungle. Play a round of mini golf after dinner, or enjoy the real thing at the Cozumel Country Club.

If your stay is a week or longer, take a trip to the mainland to see the larger ruins and nature parks. I have not included mainland activities in this book, but any of the tour operators on the Isle will be able to help you with those. Remember, the most important thing, **HAVE FUN!**

BEACHES AND BEACH CLUBS

SOUTH WEST SIDE

Dzul Ha: Probably the most popular and one of the best locations to snorkel from shore. This is a rocky shore, not sandy, but the snorkeling is so good, it is worth it. Be sure to wear beach shoes or booties, not only for the rocks, but the vast amount of sea urchins in the water. You can snorkel without going to the club right next to it, but the club has a nice patio dining area and equipment rental.

Uva's Beach club:
www.playauvas.com

A small beach area with pool, snack bar, and pool. Never crowded, so a peaceful time for relaxing. They offer all inclusive deals with food, drink, and snorkel tour.

Chankanaab Park:

A popular tourist attraction and often crowded. That said, it has a large sandy white beach for relaxing on. Good service on the beach for food and drinks, and excellent snorkeling. See Tour and activity section for further information.

Mr. Sancho's Beach
www.mrsanchos.com

This is one of my personal favorites, and my families also. Has a beautiful white beach with a pool and Jacuzzi. Bar has neat swings for seats, but be careful after a few Margaritas. Restaurant serves pretty good food at the usual inflated beach club prices. Has a group of gift shops, and I have bargained for some good prices here. There are also Horseback riding and ATV tours available from here. www.mrsanchos.com

Nachi-CoCom Beach Club:

A modern beach club with beautiful restaurant, pool and Jacuzzi and beach. They limit admission to 100 people a day to avoid overcrowding. This is an all-inclusive deal only. Please check the website for details. www.cozumelnachicocom.net

Playa Corona:

You can snorkel here and see the same things as at Chankanaab, but without the crowds. You will be one of only a few on the beach. Has a seafood restaurant and gear rental. You will need beach shoes as this is a rocky shore.

Playa San Francisco:

This is probably one of the most well-known and nicest beaches on Cozumel. It is a 3 mile long beach, with access for divers to the San Francisco and Santa Rosa reefs. Besides the beach, there is a nice pool and also a children's pool, kayak rentals and a nice restaurant, whose prices are a bit high. Also has a glass bottom tour available from here.

Paradise Beach:

A large sandy beach, with an assortment of beach toys available. Kayaks, water trampoline, and water climbing rock have a $5 fee for use of all. There is a restaurant and drinks, with service on the beach. I did not pay an admission on my last visit, but that can always change.

Playa Mia Beach Club:
www.playamiacozumel.com
011- 52 (987) 87.29.030

This club has a nice beach with plenty of beach chairs, a pool, entertainment, kid's club and a small Zoo. Entrance $15 including beach snorkel tour and most facilities. $38 includes domestic open bar too, or $49 to add a buffet, towel and snorkel gear as well.

Playa Palancar:

The most southern beach, it is seldom crowded. Avery low key atmosphere to relax in. Has Restaurant, bar gear rental, and rest Rrooms.

Playa Caletita:

Just slightly south of town, this is a small local beach area with snack bar.

Palapatita Beach Club:

Another local's beach club, with small beach and bar. Good snorkeling. Close to Papa Hogs. Entrance is free as long as you buy something. Snorkel/dive shop on site as well as a drugstore and stores selling silver and Cuban cigars.

Carlos & Charlie's Beach Club
www.carlosandcharlies.com/cozumelclub/index.htm

This is a beautiful site on a white beach next to San Francisco Beach. Good music and service.

NORTH WEST BEACHES

Beach club «Buccanos» Bar & Grill:
www.buccanos.com

You can enjoy all the beach club has to offer, including snorkeling, rock climbing and rappel park, beach side pool, jet skis, parasailing, kayaks, beach massage, lockers and a boutique There is a $10 admission which you use as food and drink credit.

Playa Azul Beach Club:

A small beach club to the north of town. Has a $5 cover charge that is applied to your food and drink. Beach, pool, bar and restaurant to help you relax and enjoy the sun.

Playa Casitas:

This public beach, Playa Casitas, is about 1 1/2 miles north of the main square and just a couple of blocks north of the airport road. There is some natural sand here and additional, fine sand has been added. There is lots of shade from the palm trees, a snack bar, and usually street vendors selling food and drink. It is very crowded on Sundays.

EAST SIDE

Mezcallito's Beach Club:

Located right at the end of the cross island road, this club can get a little wild at times, with tourists taking pictures next to the nude beach sign. Has a pretty beach for sunning, but remember swimming can be dangerous on the wild side. Good food and drinks.

Senor Iguana's Beach Club:

Friendly little place, with nice beach, gift shop, Restaurant and drinks. It is located right next to Mezcalito's. Check your meal tab carefully as there have been some reports of padded checks.

Punta Morena

This is a pretty good beach if you like to surf. Cozumel is not known for outstanding surfing but this is as good as it gets! There is a small cove where it is quite safe to swim if you are looking for an ocean dip. The beach club at Punta Morena offers food, a wading pool for the kids and change rooms.

Chen Rio Beach Club:

It is a safe beach for swimming due to the rocks breaking the waves and current. This is a popular spot with locals especially on Sundays. There is an inlet to the left side that is sandy and calm. My grandchildren like to swim and play there. Good sea food available but ask prices before you order.

Playa Bonita:

This place sits on a long stretch of quiet deserted beach, safe to swim in the shallow water. Snack bar and drinks available.

Playa San Juan:

Give this pretty nice beach area a try, where it is safe to swim and wind surf.

TOUR OPERATORS

Adventure Tours:
www.travelnotes.cc/cozumel/tours/adventure.php
This site lists many tours with direct links to the individual operators.

Best Buy Tours Cozumel
www.bestbuytourscozumel.com
011 (52) 1 987-101-4071

Locally owned, this family has been on the island for 15 years. Just send them your idea of a perfect daytrip in Cozumel and they will make sure your day turns into one of the most memorable one.

Cozumel Insider Tours & Excursions
www.cozumelinsider.com/ACTIVITIES

Cozumel tour prices on Cozumel Insider are almost always the same price as booking direct with a provider.
They do not mark up prices except in cases where charge card fees by our merchant bank require it.

Cozumel Tours (local)
www.cozumeltours.com
011-52-1-987-105-5257

Their tours are personalized at very affordable prices to clients who are visiting the island for one day or for longer stays at the hotels, villas and condos. Check out the list of tours that they offer, and if you want to create something different, send them an e-mail with your ideas, and they will tailor a tour just for you and your family and friends

Cozumel Tours.Com
www.cozumel-tours.com
866-464-6205

Johan and Sandra offer a "Fun Card" with the purchase of any tour. The "Fun Card" card can be used as many times as you want during your vacation, saving you up to 30% at over 45 locations throughout Cozumel, including Restaurants, Shopping and more! Owners are not located on the island.

Island Holidays Travel Agency
www. islandholidaystravel agency.com
Ave 5 between Calle 2 & 4

Looking for things to do in Cozumel? Travel, Lodging, Tours information and Accommodation for Cozumel, including Cancun, Playa del Carmen, the Mayan Riviera, well… You have come to the right place. I know this staff personally and trust them completely. They will soon be a fully certified travel agency and can take care of all your travel needs.

This is Cozumel
www. thisiscozumel.com
214-556-6651

They offer a large inventory of over 50 tours on their web site. If you are a cruise ship passenger and your ship changes itinerary, your refund is guaranteed.

Two D's Diving and Tour Adventures
www.2dsdivingandtours.com
011 52 987 - 120 0730

Deanna Campbell came to visit us in Cozumel a couple of years ago and she never left. She has turned her love of the island into a thriving and well-reviewed business. They are an intimate operation that provides a personal and professional vacation for you and your family.
Their goal is to give you a safe and memorable experience that will last for a lifetime. They offer everything from diving to special requested tours that are not listed. Highly rated, read their reviews on Trip advisor. **Deanna is offering our readers a 10% discount with our coupon on scuba diving, snorkeling tour, private and customized tours.**

Note: *I have only listed tour companies that I, my family, or my friends have had an experience with. If a tour company is not listed, it does not mean there is anything wrong with them.*

INDIVIDUAL TOURS & ACTIVITIES

I list direct links to some tours, but for others you may have to use a tour operator.

Amazing Cozumel Race!

You'll need your wits, your energy, and your willingness to have fun as you race the clock and each other in an attempt to be the first team to unlock the code and defeat an ancient «Mayan Curse». This is a great way to have fun while sight-seeing. $79

Atlantis Adventures
www.atlantisadventures.com
011-52-987-872-5671

If you would like to experience the Magical underwater wonderland of Cozumel, and you do not dive, well this one's for you. This is a real US Coast Guard certified submarine. Go to depths of 100 ft. and get an up-close viewing of the tropical sea life that Cozumel is famous for. Sub is air conditioned and small children are allowed. Cost is $89 adult and $59 for children 12 and under, or 36 inches tall.

ATV Wild Tour:
www.wild-tours.com/atv-all-terrain-vehicles.html

ATV thru the jungle, a great fun ATV ride in lush green flora, exploring ancient Mayan sites.
$65 single $115 double $90 with child 6–11

Caballito del Caribe Pirate Ship
www.seahorsecozumel.com
011-52-987-872-1449

Offers sunset cruises and Pirates night. Serves lobster dinner. Also Snorkeling tours. I have done the pirate ship several times and always look forward to going again. My whole family from age 2 to age 60 love this tour. The steak is amazingly tender and the lobster sweet. It is fun for adults and kids alike. Adults: $70-79, Kids over 7 $40-45, Kids under 7 free but $15 if meal requested.

Gina and the Pirates

Caribbean Bol
Calle 13 between Ave 5 & Gonzalo Guerrero
staceydianne@yahoo.com
011-52-987-878-4321

Go bowling at Cozumel's only bowling alley. This provides an alternative to the Island's water sports and is also great in-door fun on rainy days with board games, video games, and billiards offered upstairs for those who don't bowl. Games are $3-4.50 depending on day and time. Shoes are $2 and pool is $6 per hour. Bring in our coupon from "Cozumel the Complete Guide II" and get a free game!!!

Chankanaab Park:
www.cozumelparks.org.mx

Besides the beach and snorkeling there are other activities her. Tour the beautiful gardens and view the replicas of Mayan artifacts. Swim with the dolphins, manatees, or watch the sea lion show. Some activities have separate admission. Admission is $19, child $12

Chocolates Kaokao Tour
www.chocolateskaokao.com
011-52-987- 869-4705
Salas between Ave 80 & 85

Learn about the history of cocoa, its importance in the world of the ancient Maya. Learn how it is harvested, processed, and, sample the chocolate! Watch the whole process from bean- to- bar, that includes roasting the cocoa beans, grinding it into the stone mill «molino», temper the cocoa paste and mold the chocolate! After the tour, visitors will have the chance to purchase Kaokao products at the factory store. Admission is free.

Cine Cozumel:
www.cinepolis.com/_CARTELERA/cartelera.aspx?ic=53

This is a Local modern movie theater located in the Chedraui shopping complex near Calle 11 and Melgar. Movies are in English with Spanish sub titles, except for children's productions. Cost is way below what itis in the US, about $5 U.S.

Climbing Adventure Park
2 Miles North of town

I have been unable to locate a direct link for this activity, but the tour is offered by several tour operators. Operated by the Alaska Mountain Guides from Haines, Alaska, the park has several climbing walls, a short zip line, abseiling towers and a nice beach club for snorkeling afterwards. About $60

Cozumel Bar Hop
www.cozumelbarhop.com
011-52-987-872-2294

Why take a chance by drinking and driving? This tour solves that dilemma by providing you with a designated driver who is both bilingual and knowledgeable about the island. Grab some friends and jump on this bus that takes you to four of the "wild side" bars. You will visit Punta Morena, Coconuts, Playa Bonita & Rastas and receive a free shot to start each visit. Bring your camera for the beautiful scenery and life long memories. **Get a FREE "Cozumel Bar Hop" tee shirt when you present the coupon in this book**.
5 hours for $49, cheaper than a private taxi!

Cozumel Country Club Golfing
www.cozumelcountryclub.com.mx:
011-52-987-872-9579
Carreterra Costera Norte, 6.5 km

A fairly new 18 hole par 72 Championship course.
$169 including cart $105 after 1 pm Specials are offered online.

Cozumel Kiteboarding
www.cozumelkiteboarding.com
adrian@cozumelkiteboarding.com

Because we are committed to fun now you can come to Cozumel and experience one of a kind Kiteboarding vacation!! Great winds year round and long sandy beaches are the perfect scenery combined with the warm crystal clear waters makes of Cozumel a great place to get to the extreme excitement or just fully relax. **Purchase a Kiteboard from Puro Mar Surf-Kite-Bikini Shop and get a free lesson with coupon.**

Cozumel Mini Golf:
Calle 1 & Ave 15
Mini golf in the middle of tropical garden, complete with waterfalls and iguanas. A challenging course, believe me I embarrassed myself. Order cerveza, sangria and soda by walkie-talkie. $7

Cozumel Sailing:
www.cozumelsailing.com
011-52-987-869-2312
864-724-5464

Sailing and snorkel tours, barefoot sailboat rental, sunset sails. Owned and operated by Capt. Dan and his First Mate Juan, you are sure to have a great time with them no matter which activity you choose. A favorite of mine and others is the Toucan tour, includes a sailing trip, fishing, a grilled lunch, drinks, and spinnaker rides, kind of Para— sailing in place. My bunch of teens had a blast.
Tucan $90 adults $45 children, Contact for private charter and barefoot sailing prices.

Cozumel Surfing
www.cozumelsurfing.com
011-52-1- 987-111-9290

If you want to try surfing while in Mexico "Cozumel Surfing" is the way to go. Nacho makes the lessons fun and you get plenty of rides. If you are staying in Cozumel I definitely recommend you try surfing with Nacho! Whatever your needs are, Nacho can make it happen.
They have long boards, short boards and boogie boards.

Discover Scuba: Introduction to scuba includes 1 dive. $50-100, this is available at most hotels and dive operations.

Dolphinaris Cozumel
www.dolphinaris.com/locations/cozumel.aspx
Melgar between Calles 17 & 19
800-365-7446

These dolphins are located right in town. It is the only thing they do so there is no park admission. Programs run from $74 to $189. You can often find discount promotions on the web site.

Dolphin Discovery Cozumel
www.dolphindiscovery.com/cozumel
Chankanaab Park
866-393-5158

Since they are located in the park you must pay park admission in addition to any program you participate in. In addition to the dolphin programs they also have a manatee program and a sea lion discovery.

Rates start at $49 for the manatees and sea lions and go as high as $199to dive with the dolphins.

Dune Buggy Tour:
www.cozumeldunebuggytours.com
011-52- 987- 872-3204
USA 918- 747- 8160

Beach tour, Mayan ruins, snorkeling, picnic lunch.
The two tour guides Omar and Antonio are bilingual and they take special care to make sure you have a great adventure.
Access isolated beach areas accessible by dune buggy or water only.
$99 adult $49.50 child 3–8 under 3 free

Spinniker ride on the Tucan

El Cedral: This is the oldest Maya Structure on Cozumel, built A.D. 800, it is a small ruin, located at the very first town on Cozumel. You will find some small shops and a place for snacks. It is a few miles south on the beach road,. During the last weekend in April there is a large fiesta.

El Cementerio (The Cemetery)
At the south end of downtown's El Centro neighborhood, a 7 block walk from the downtown plaza, you'll find the old cemetery. Walk down the waterfront to the Post Office. Turn up Calle 7 and walk one block up to Ave 5. There are some very interesting grave sites and mausoleums. FREE

El Museo:
www.cozumelparks.org.mx

A lovely museum with a lot of information about the history of Cozumel, located on the waterfront street, Melger between Calle 4 & 6.
Tour the Museum and then have lunch on the balcony.
$5, online special $3
Schedules: Mo, Tu, We, Th, Fr & Sat
Times: From 9:00 a.m. to 5:00 p.m. local time (CST)

Fly High Adventures
www.cozumelflyhighadventures.com
http://www.youtube.com/watch?v=rv2z-RFlgg4
5 minutes South of International pier

Fly high Adventures Zip Line Park is located at the southern part of Cozumel Island. Wooden towers built over the jungle; there is more than 2,500 ft. on12 different length zip lines varying speeds on lines.
The park is surrounded by jungle teeming with exotic wild life and plants, with the highest towers in the park offer stunning views.
Contact them for prices and specials. **Enjoy a refreshing drink afterwards for free, with coupon in this book.**

Fury Catamarans
www.furycozumel.com
011-52-987-872-5145

Popular for its snorkel, sail, and beach party tour, with lunch and all you can drink. The owners have run the Fury tour for many years and it has become a Cozumel staple. My daughter and son enjoy the dancing and partying on the return trip. Snorkel and beach party is $59 + 2.10 Snorkel only is $45+2.10

Island Tour: A guided tour around the Island includes ruins site, shopping, swimming, and a visit to wild east side. Depending how many hours and what you want to do, tour companies charge $40 to $75 per person. Another option is to make a bargain with a van or taxi driver who speaks good English and rent the cab for anywhere from $40 for 2 people to $100 for the van.

Jungle Horse Tour: Ride into the Mayan jungle, visits the oldest town on Cozumel at the El Cedral ruins. 2 1/2 hours $32 age 8 or older only.
This is available from most tour operators.

Jungle Jeep Tour: Jungle and snorkel tour. Fascinating ruins, awesome snorkeling, Breakfast rolls, snacks, lunch and drinks. I have personally enjoyed this tour, it was great, and especially for those who get to drive. 5 hrs. $85

Jungle Trek: A hiking tour led by an experienced guide, includes swimming time. 3–4 hrs. over 4 miles. $45 + $3 insurance

Lagoon, Nature, and Bird Watching Tour

Bird watching tour on Cozumel Island is available from several tour operators.. This tour is designed especially for nature lovers and beginner bird watchers. Cost is usually $129

Mr. Sancho's Beach Club:
www.mrsanchos.com/mr_sanchos/home.htm
Horseback riding on the beach and ATV tours in the jungle,
Approximately $30 an hour.

Paco's Kiteboarding
www.pacoskiteboarding.com
surfpacos@hotmail.com
http://facebook.com/surfpacos

Paco Chan is a PASA-certified kiteboarding instructor and is also a PADI Dive master.
Private instruction $125 per hour (min. 3 hrs.)
(one-to-one) $500 per day
Commitment Course 3 days - $900 per student

Recommended for beginners who are serious about becoming a kite boarder.
Group of 2 students $300 per day each

All instruction includes gear and personal water craft support if needed. Instruction starts at 10am and finishes at 4pm with a relaxing break for lunch. Paco also offers something really different! Kiteboarding tours around the island, include transport, drinks, lunch and stoked riding with Paco.

15% off instruction and 10 % off tours when you give Paco the coupon in this book and tell him Patricia sent you.

PARASAILING
www.cozumelwatersports.com/ToursExcursions/Parasailing.htm

Parasailing is provided along Cozumel's western shore, and boats can be flagged down from the hotel area south of San Miguel and at San Francisco Beach. "Cozumel Water Sports" seems to offer the best price with longer air times. It is $50 for 13-15 minutes and $90 for tandems.

Passion Island Beach Break
www.isla-pasion.com/all-inclusive-beach-tour-cozumel.html

This is an all-inclusive tour. You get transportation, a private beach, open bar, buffet, beach activities, and a children's area. Adults are $65, children $40, and under age 4 are free.

Punta Molas Lighthouse with Adrian
especiascozumel@hotmail.com

This is probably the most awesome tour on the Island. You need to go To adviser and read the reviews and descriptions. You must be in good physical shape to do this tour. You will see sights that most people never get to see, and snorkel where no one else does. Adrian's sandwiches are nothing to laugh at either. $250 for 2 people, $80 each additional up to 5 passengers. Be sure to contact Adrian far in advance.

Punta Sur
www.cozumelparks.org.mx

An ecological park designed for educating visitors. Nesting turtles program, ruins, lagoons, and the Punta Celerain Lighthouse. Located on the southern tip of the island, Punta Sur is the largest natural eco reserve on Cozumel Island with more than 2,700 acres. Enjoy the beautiful beach, climb up the Celarain lighthouse, take photos of crocodiles, exotic birds, fish and flowers. A catamaran boat ride by the lagoon is included, Adults are $10 and children are $5.

Rancho Buenavista:
www.buenavistaranch.com
011-52-987-872-1537

Saddle up and enjoy guided tour on horseback thru the jungle and visits to several Mayan ruins. They also do a really nice sunset ride, but be sure to bring a good bug spray.

San Gervasio Ruins:
www.cozumelparks.org.mx

Located On cross island road approximately 7 km outside of the city. Not as big as the mainland sites, but still very interesting. This is where the Mayan women came from the mainland to worship. San Gervasio was a sacred Mayan site dedicated to the goddess Ixchel (goddess of fertility) plus a strategic site for commerce and politics in the area.
$5 at the gate and $3 online

Stingray Beach Cozumel
www.stingraybeach.com
987-872-4932
1 mile south of town on Melgar
Spend some quality time with these friendly stingrays. Expert guides teach you how to interact with these remarkable animals. There is a reason all of the reviews are positive; the place is great; friendly employees, clean facilities, and an awesome experience. This is a very safe experience for all ages. Unlike swimming with the stingrays in Grand Cayman, these stingrays are contained in a penned area and are barb-free. Children $34 Adults $59 Child

Sunday In the Plaza:
Enjoy the bands, dance with your sweetie, or just sit and relax. This is a wonderful evening of people watching. Stroll around and enjoy the snacks offered by vendors. Bring candy and hand it out to the children. Not to be missed if you are in town on a Sunday evening. During high season and holidays you will find the same activities Friday-Sunday.

176

Temazcal the Mayan Steam Bath
www.temazcalcozumel.com/temazcal.html

Completely isolated and hidden in the middle of the jungle, far away from the noise and stress emerges Xkan-Ha Reserve. The temazcal were used widely among the Aztecs and Mayan that populated Mesoamerica and for centuries and as far back as can be traced was a therapeutic instrument, an arm of the medical practice. You will emerge a totally new person. $80 adults only

Tequila Tour Cozumel Hacienda Antigua:
www.facebook.com/pages/Tequila-Tour-Cozumel-Hacienda-Antigua
011-52- 987 869 46 77

Along the cross island road that leads to its Eastern Shore you will pass the Tequila Hacienda, where you can partake in a Tequila History Tour if you so desire. Each tour includes the opportunity to taste several types of tequila. The cost is $18 and well worth it.

Club 21

COZUMEL NIGHT LIFE

Although it isn't a party town when compared to Cancun or even Playa del Carmen, there is some night life to be found. The clubs tend to stay open until the wee hours of the morning, so if you plan on party time, then take a day off from diving the next day.

Ambar Bar & Lounge
Ave 5 #141 Pedestrian walkway off Plaza
987-869-1955

It is a more upscale bar than others. When you're passing by it looks small inside, but there's a large courtyard in the back w/ tables outside. They have a live rock band "Cenicero" Wednesdays thru Saturdays from 11 PM to 3 AM.

Carlos and Charlie's:
11 Melger Ave
011-52-987-872-0191

The same wild party that goes on in every port this chain is located.
There is loud music, Tex-Mex food, and plenty of dancing.

Casino Club 21
Calle 7# 398 between Ave 20 & 25
open 11AM-3AM, 7 days/wk.

This is a gaming room with 2 floors of video slots and electronic BJ tables, Texas Hold'Em, & Roulette tables. If you haven't been by to see the place, these are good reasons to visit at least once. It's Cozumel's new adult entertainment. In addition to some fun betting there is a fresh water swimming pool and a very attractive (with real grass) courtyard...you are invited to enjoy those for free and you are welcome to bring your kids. They must remain outside of the gaming area, but they have a fun and supervised area for them to play and generally offer them free soft drinks. Drinks for adults are cheap and often comped; beer is always 2 for 1. Food is sandwiches and baskets at very reasonable prices. **Use our coupon and get 2 free drinks with any play credit.**

Corona Sports Bar
www. coronasportsbar.weebly.com
Between Casa Denis and Melody on Calle 1 in the Plaza

Good drink prices, food available and a rocking house band "Kaoba" make this a fun place to party. If you're looking for a great cheese burger, a game of pool, a live band, a place to watch the NFL, NHL, NBA, and more, then the Corona Sports Bar is your place.

Hard Rock Cafe:
2A Melger Ave
011-52-987-872-5271

The smallest Hard Rock in the world, it makes up for it in Ear shattering music. It is loads of fun for Hard Rock Café fans. The house band is pretty good.

Havana Club:
Melgar between Calles 6 and 8, 2nd fl
011-52-987-872-1268

For great jazz, good company, drinks, and great cigars, check out the Havana Club.

La Hach
Across from Villa Blanca Hotel

Sam and Alex are a friendly couple who run this great place. Good food and drinks enjoyed in great company. They have a rock band Wednesdays thru Sundays. "Karma" is super fun to dance to as are the other bands that play here. This is also another place to watch the beautiful sunset, especially on the top deck. **Present our coupon and receive 15% off your bill. Not available during happy hours**.

Pirata's
http://es-la.facebook.com/piratascozumel
Ave 5 between Salas & Calle 1

Pirata's provides it all, great food, fun and music, $1 Coronas and different daily drinks specials. Live music that goes LATE Thursday (Reggae), Friday and Saturday (Rock) in this casual atmosphere is nothing short of a fantastic night out

Room Service
Melgar between Margaritaville and Punta Langosta

This is one of the most popular clubs with locals now. It has 3 floors playing different kinds of music with a bar on each floor! The place really jumps after midnight.

Senor Frogs
11 Melger Ave

Another version of Carlos and Charlie's, and located above them, but more locals and more fun. Just hop on the escalator and ride on up. If the M.C. Daniel is there be nice to him, he's my nephew.

The Money Bar
www.facebook.com/group.php?gid=52549979024
At Dzul Ha on old beach road
987- 869-5141

"The Red Eye Band" plays from 6 - 9 Fridays through Sundays and they are not to be missed!!! They are one of my favorite bands anywhere and really get the place rocking. Be prepared to dance the night away while enjoying the beautiful sunset as a backdrop!!

Tiki Tok
Melgar between Calle 2 & 4 second on floor

Bamboo ceilings, an imported beach and an awesome Salsa band make Tiki Tok one of the best places to enjoy Salsa on Cozumel. One of my best friends and a great Salsa dancer can often be found heating up the floor. Music starts at 11 pm.!

Viva México
Av. Rafael E. Melgar
872-0799

This dance club that has a DJ who spins Latin and American dance music until the wee hours. Gets loud and crowded, but lots of fun. No connection to the Viva Mexico restraint..

MEXICAN CANTINAS

Just a quick word about these local Mexican bars. Although they are not really considered a part of the night life as they open early afternoon and normally close at 6 pm. Some of them do stay open later into the evening.

They are fun places to hear local music, enjoy inexpensive beer and drinks, and eat FREE food. Yes I said FREE. All cantinas serve snacks called "botanas" which can be anything from fried chicken wings or fish to something's you cannot identify. Try the weird stuff anyway, it is often very good.

I will give you a short list of the cantinas I am familiar with or someone I know is familiar with. There over 100 cantinas on the island, some of which you do not want to enter. My advice is to go with someone who knows the place, or ask your dive master to go out with you.

Cachocas on Calle 4 between 15 & 20

Chindos on Ave 40 between 3 & 7

El Camaron on Ave 65 between 19 & 21

El Fish on the corner of Calle 8 and 10

El Gato Negro on Calle 6 between Ave 25 & 20
This is the local gathering place for expatriates and visitors on Friday afternoons. The chicken wings get me there as often as possible

El Pioline on the corner of 3 South and 15

Las Boyas on Calle 3 between Ave 15 & 20
There is a waiter here named Jose who I think is the owner's brother. You must ask him to sing with the band. I have listened to him for over 10 years and I cannot get enough. He sings like an angel.

Las Brisas on Calle 5 between 15 & 20

Migualitos on Calle 5 between 25 & 30

Ronulfos on Ave 10 & Calle 5

OK, this is for those single guys out there! Cozumel does have *"Gentlemen's Clubs"*.

I will not list them as I do not feel comfortable doing that. I just wanted to say that they are here and any taxi driver or local can direct you to them. BE CAREFUL!

CHAPTER X

MONEY-MEDICAL
CHURCH & SPECIALTY
SERVICES

Everything you may need on vacation.

MEDICAL, BANKING, CHURCHES, AND SPECIAL SERVICES

MEDICAL

The Medical care available in Cozumel is very good. There are hospitals, clinics, and Doctors who speak English and can provide excellent care. In the event of a catastrophic emergency you can be air evacuated to the US. I became severely ill with pneumonia and received outstanding care at the CMC clinic/hospital. I know others who have spent several days of their vacation in this hospital and received the same level of care.

Also available are Dentists, (people often save their dental work for here as the work is excellent and the prices low), a Chiropractor, hyperbaric chambers, and opticians. Please be aware that you will be expected to pay cash or credit card at most places and file with your insurance at home.

HOSPITALS AND CLINICS

CMC (Centro Medico de Cozumel) located on Calle 1. It's open 24 hrs., English speaking doctors, very modern, laboratory, air ambulance, associated with Miami hospital, air-evac, professional and friendly service. Phones 987/872-5664, 987/872-3370, 987/872-3545

Clinica San Miguel
Clinic offering emergency care
Small three bed clinic offering 24-hour emergency care. Specializes in pediatrics. Emergency room with modern equipment available and there are some English-speaking doctors.
Calle 6, 133 (between Ave 5 & 10 9872-0103

Cruz Roja
This is another excellent choice for inexpensive quality care. Intestinal problems, stitches, sprains, etc. Can easily be handled by this great staff.
Ave 65 & Calle 25   872-1058

Hospital General
This is a small hospital where mostly Spanish is spoken, but they will find someone to translate if needed. This is a much less expensive option for simple things. I have

used them several times as have my family members. Lab tests, xrays, and simple consultations are amazingly cheap.
Calle 11 & Ave 20   987 8725182

Clinica CEM: 872-2919
Clinica Medica del Sur: 872-5787
Social Security Hospital: 872-0140
IMSS: 872-0222
Clinica Villanueva: 872-0395
Clinica Guadalupe: 872-2508

Quiropráctico de Cozumel: Avenida 5 between Calle 3 and 5: 872-5099
There is an excellent chiropractor, Dr. Scott Kircher. He speaks English fluently and is knowledgeable in Spanish. He practices some unique "holistic" healing that amaze those in pain. He won't pop your bones if you don't want him to, but he will still help you.

COZUMEL HEALTH - CREW BODY SHOP
Plaza Barracuda / Hotel Barracuda Building
Phone: 987-872-1122

Chiropractic, Acupuncture, Sports Medicine, Physical Therapy, Massage, Lower Back, Chronic Pain Specialist. Tell Dr. Joe that I sent you; maybe he will give me a break on my regular visits.

Camera Hyperbaric: 872-1430
This is Cozumel's hyper baric chamber used mainly for diving accidents but has been known to help stroke victims as well. The hospital has X-ray machines and more. Dr. Pascual Piccolo is the resident doctor. They work well with Americans and are fluent in both languages.

DOCTORS

DR. RECHY	872-2182
DR. JESUS MATEOS	872-5787
DR. JORGE ALVAREZ	872-2534
DR. LEWIS	872-1616
DR. PICCOLO	872-3070
DR.SERGOVIA	872-3545
DR. MORALES	044-987-876-0666 CELL

DR. PADILLA	044-987-878-5161 CELL
Cardiologist	
Dr. Jorge Alvarez	Cell: 876-0808, office: 872-2534

DENTISTS

Dr. Arteta
Calle 11 between Ave 35 & 45
044-987-100-1576 cell
987 107 8720

He speaks fluent English, all areas of dentistry including oral surgery.
He has been our family dentist for over 10 years. Try getting an implant for $1000 in the USA!

Dra.Yazmin Ibrahim-Mohamed Alfie
11 Av. con 65 AV.
Tel: (987)8720808 ext. 107
yazmin_ibrahim@hotmail.com

This is another very popular dentist. I have only heard good things about her and many of the local expats use her.

Dr. Hernandez	872-0656
Dr. Mariles	872-1352
Dr. Luis Angel	872-0808
Dr. Miguel Peraza Peniche	calle 3 between 25 & 30

PHARMACIES

There are pharmacies on every corner in Cozumel. Many of our RX in the USA do not require a prescription here, except for the controlled drugs, such as narcotics. As of recently you must now get a written RX for antibiotics. This can be done for about 30 pesos at the Similares locations. The pharmacist expects you to know what you need, and will loan you his PDA drug guide. Your best bet is to either look up the Spanish name before leaving home, or go to the American pharmacy where they can tell you the correct name. A short list of pharmacies is listed here, but that does not mean the others are not OK.

American Discount Drugstore
Medication at Bargain Prices English Spoken
Tel: (9) 872-4855

Los colores de Dori
2 North between Rafael E. Melgar & 5th Avenue
872-2238

El Kiosco
5th Street at 1st south
872-2485

Dori
5th Avenue at 7 south
872-5519

Paris
6th North between 5th and 10th North
872-3552

Portal del parque
5th Avenue South in between Juárez Avenue & 1st South
869-2119

Pharmacia Joaquin
5th & Plaza del sol Ave
872-0195

La Placita
Juárez Avenue between 5th & 10th
872-5132

Portales
11th Avenue between Rafael E. Melgar & 5th Avenue
872-0936

Portales
10th Avenue #101 between Juárez
872-1048

Farmacia Similares
Ave 15 & Calle 1
Ave 30 (Coldwell) between Calle 19 & 21
Ave 90 & Calle 3

This chain specializes in generic drugs and the prices are usually the lowest. Attached to each is a small clinic where you can see a doctor and get an RX for 30 pesos.

Yza
5th Avenue between Juárez & 2nd North #50
872-2777

OPTICIANS AND EYE GLASSES

Dra. Concepción Planas Fernández
Calle 6 between Melgar and 5 Ave, south side of the street
872-3805

She has a totally computerized system and does a thorough eye exam herself as well. She also does Botox and other anti-aging injections at a very reasonable price.

OptiCon
Ave 10 between Calle 7 and Calle 9

Has a fair selection of frames at reasonable prices.

Optica DaVinci
65 #264 entre 12Y14nte
Cell-987-105-2701

ENGLISH AA MEETINGS 6 pm daily 872-3836
Calle 5 & Ave 10

MONEY AND BANKING

There are a number of banks in Cozumel where you can exchange currency. Your resort or hotel may also offer exchange services, but their rates may not be as good. Convenience sometimes costs a bit more. There are also money exchanges and ATMs as well.

Santander Bank
10th Avenue #198 at the corner of 3rd Street
872-2853

If you have a Bank of America account this is the bank to use. There will be no charges by either bank. It is also a good idea to set up "safe send" with BOA before you leave. You can then wire money at no charge to yourself. This is the only location but they do have an ATM at the airport between the arrival and departure terminals.

Banamex
5th Avenue at Calle 1 & A. R. Salas
872-3411

Bancomer
5th Avenue at Plaza del Sol
872-0550

Banorte
5th Avenue between Juárez & 2nd North
872-0718

HSBC
Ave 30 & Calle 11
Juarez between Ave 10 & 15

ATM MACHINES

You can find an ATM on every corner in the main town square. Keep in mind that the machines delivers pesos not U.S. dollars. There is only one place to go if you need to make an advance on your credit card and want US$...BANAMEX downtown just inside the main town square when entering from 5th Avenue and Adolfo Rosado Salas. My advice is to use only the machines that are located attached to a bank, during banking hours. That way if there is a problem you can resolve it immediately. Using ATMs is usually the best bang for the buck. The exchange rates are better than the money exchanges and even better than the banks. There are ATMs all around town and also at the Mega and Chedraui stores.

Cozumel Money Exchanges

Like a bank, money exchanges can convert your current currency at the going rate in pesos. You may get a slightly better rate from one to the next, or even at one of the banks. Check around. It is a good idea to be familiar with the exchange rate before you go! These places are located all over Cozumel, but I list a few to get you started.

Asesores turísticos y cambiarios
5th Ave # 121
872-0276

Consultaría internacional
Calle 1 & Plaza Confetti
872-4480

Diamond exchange
R. E. Melgar # 111
872-2043

Monex
Av. Juárez $
10th Avenue

CHURCH SERVICES

CATHOLIC CHURCHES

Parroquia San Miguel 10th Avenue at Ave Juárez

Corpus Christi 20th Avenue between 15 and 17th St.

Iglesia de Guadalupe 65th Avenue at 8th Street North

PRESBYTERIAN SERVICES

Templo Evangelico Presbiteriano Juarez Avenue between 40 & 45th St.

Nueva Iglesia Presbiteriana 11th Avenue at 90th Street

Ebenezer Presbyterian
Ave Pedro Joaquin Coldwell between 8 and 10
ENGLISH SERVICES ON SUNDAY AT 9AM
872-3400

GREEK ORTHODOX
EBEN EZER P.J. Coldwell between 8 and 10th Street North.

Non-Denominational Christian In English
Calle 11 between Ave 15 & 20

Jehovah Witness 2 locations
Ave 65 between Calle 7 & 9
Calle Rosado Salas

Church of Jesus Christ
Ave 40 and Calle 4
872-4167

Church of Latter Day Saints
Calle 4 and about 45 AV

Chabad of Cozumel (Jewish)
Calle 12 between Melgar and Ave 5, Las Iguanas
(305) 432-2406 U.S Line 1
(516) 596-8906 U.S Line 2
Cell: +52 (987) 111-9715 Rabbi Dudi Caplin,
Cell: +52 (987) 117-9518 Rabbi Shlomi Peleg
Email: ChabadCozumel@gmail.com
Website: http://www.chabadcozumel.com/
Rabbi David Nechemia Hacohen Caplin, dudi770@gmail.com

INTERNET AND CALLING STATIONS

Do NOT use the red phones that you see everywhere on the island. These are VERY, VERY expensive and you will regret it!

There are calling stations and Internet cafes all over the city, and in the neighborhoods. Here are a few to help if you can't seem to find them.

Diamond Internet Café
Ave 10 #200 between Calle 4 & 6
9am–9pm Mon-Sat

THE CALLING STATION
Ave Rafael Melgar at Calle 3
Long distance phone calls and fax service.
Open 7 days a week.

The Coffee Net
Melger & Calle 11,
You can check your e-mail (through Netscape, AOL, and Hot Mail,
among others

Many places also have free wireless if you have your laptop, Ipad, Smartphone, or
E-Reader with you. Download Skype and use it and the wireless to make free calls.

Laundry NET
Ave 30 (Coldwell) between Calle 6&8
Monday - Saturday 8 am - 9 pm, Sunday 9 am – Noon

Laundry Net is both a Laundromat and Internet service provider. You
can catch up on your email and uploading your pictures while your
laundry is going.

LAUNDRY SERVICE OR SELF SERVICE

Laundry prices usually run $10 to $15 pesos per kilo.

Laundry NET- see above internet description.

Lavanderia Express—872-2932
Adolfo Rosado Salas between Calle 5 & Calle 10. Coin operated.

Lavanderia Mañana—Calle 11 in Plaza Los Arcos Drop off & pick up.

Lavanderia Margarita—872-2865
Ave 20 between Adolfo Rosado Salas & Calle 3. Drop off and pick up.

Tintoreria Del Mar—872-5470
Ave 20 between Adolfo Rosado Salas & Calle 1. Reliable dry cleaning is available.

Lavanderia Rosita—872-1262
Calle 40 & Hidalgo—Drop off and pick up.

MASSAGE AND SPA SERVICES

ACQUA SPA
www.acquaspa.com.mx
987-872-7192
Carret. Costera Sur Km 2.4 Villa Sur

Offers massage, wraps, facials, manicures, and pedicures. Try the chocolate body wrap for a "sweet" time.

BAREFOOT IN COZUMEL
www.barefootincozumel.com
011-52-987-878-4662

Owned and operated by Sally Hurwitch, I can vouch personally for her skills, ahhh it feels so good. A practitioner of Swedish massage, Reiki, and Ashiatsu Bar Therapy for 15 years, she practices in the quiet peaceful surroundings of her island cottage. She has been rated the #1 massage therapist in Cozumel by "Cozumel Islander Magazine". Rates start @ $60 per hour. **Receive 10% off on your massage with Sally's coupon in this book.**

COZUMEL MASSAGE
http://davidmechlin.com/work/cozumelmassage/index.html
Out-calls only
Helen@cozumelmassage.com

Owned and operated by Helen Green who was trained in London England. Helen trained in several different styles of massage, and also offers hair and makeup services. Helen says; " When you book a massage, we will make arrangements for me to come to your home, villa, or hotel (selected hotels only). I bring the table, soothing music, and other equipment to you. I have found this to be easiest for me; most comfortable and hassle-free for the client."

COZUMEL SPA
www.cozumelspa.com
Carretera Costera Sur KM 3.8 Local # 1 Palmar Condos
987-872-66 15

The spa offers a wide array of services. The one that intrigues me is "the total body system". If anyone of you tries this PLEASE email me a report. They are getting good reviews.

SPA Del SOL
www.spadelsolcozumel.com
Calle 5 #34, Melgar and Ave 5
011-52- 987 872 6474

With 18 years of experience in all areas of massage and beauty treatments, this spa, with a holistic approach, not only performs every spa treatment I can think of, they also perform and instruct in an assortment of alternative medicine. Acupuncture, traditional chiropractic, and ear candling are but a few that you can choose from. They continuously offer discounts and packages that make affordable their professional treatments.**They will offer 15% off on any treatment, except packages, when the person shows the coupon from "Cozumel the Complete Guide II".**

BEAUTY SALONS: You can expect to pay anywhere from $8.00 to $20.00 for a cut at most island shops. Manicures are priced around $6.00 and up

BluBambu Salon & Spa
Calle 15 Between Ave 10 & 15
katie@blubambumx.com
987-103- 8854

BluBambu Salon & Spa is a full service salon; they don't just cut or color your hair. BluBambu Salon & Spa offers a full range of nail care services, including manicures and pedicures and can assist you with make-up techniques, hair styling.

Barney's
Ave 7 between 18th and 20th Streets San Miguel II
Cuts, color, manicure, pedicure at economical prices

Don Cabello
Corner of Ave 20 and 25TH Street
Cuts, color, manicure
Limited English Spoken

Estetica Imagen
In the Chedraui Mall
987- 869- 7639

This is a full service beauty salon for women, children, and men. Walk in clients are welcome!

Island Creations
Ave 50 between 14th and 16th Streets
Cuts, color, eyebrow wax
By appointment Tele: 872-6284
English Spoken

Kenny Villanueva—La Estetica
Av. Juarez and 55th Ave

Cuts, foils, highlights, color, pedicure, manicure, body massage English Spoken

Sandra's Beauty Salon
Ave 10 diagonally across from Kelley's Bar
987-103-0787

Sandra speaks very little English, but she is worth the extra effort to show her what you want. This Gal gave me the best haircut and style I have ever had. She was the first to understand what I had been looking for. My cost was $100 MP about $8.50 USD.

FLORISTS

Floreria Evelyn 872-4028
65 AV between Calles 16 & 18

They offer beautiful flowers, buy a bunch or have an arrangement created very inexpensively.

Floreria Mariela 872-7686
1st Street between 15 & 20 Avenues

Fast, friendly service with arrangements and bouquets created as you wait. They carry fresh, long stemmed roses of every color imaginable that the owner keeps in a back room, just ask to see them.

Floreria Paraiso 872-3389
Ave 25 between Salas & Calle 3

They also offer beautiful flowers at great prices. They are FTD members if you need to send flowers home for a special occasion.

WEDDING PLANNERS

Cozumel Wedding Planner
www.cozumelweddingplanner.com
Info@cozumelweddingplanner.com
011-52-987-872-4878

Make your special day a stress free one. Leave the planning to Stephanie, who has been planning Cozumel weddings for many years.

SOMETHING SPECIAL
www.cozumelmexico.net/wedding-services
011-52-987-872-5857

Fiona Anne Lomax will plan your wedding from a simple basic ceremony to a wedding spectacular.

VIDEO RENTALS

BLOCK BUSTER
Juarez & Ave 30

Offers most movies in English, except children's productions. Just sign up for free and it works the same as in the U.S.

CALLING STATION
Melger waterfront

Offers a small assortment of English movies and video players for rent.

CAMERA AND FILM SERVICES

ISLAND PHOTO AND VIDEO CENTER
www.islacozumel.net/services/armando
At the entrance to La Ceiba Hotel
011-52-987-872-5833

This is a full service photo lab. They do custom video production; give instruction in underwater photography and videography. They also have rental equipment available.

Foto Omega
Melger & Calle 3

They offer developing and printing in minutes for 35MM, APS, or Digital Media. Experienced in working with English-speaking clients and offers a wide range of services. Expect to pay about 90 pesos to
develop a 35mm, 24-exposure roll of film.

Fujifilm/ColorMax
Ave Juarez between 25 and 30 (across from the gas station)

Popular with locals and offers more reasonable prices than Omega, Fuji is a full-service operation offering cameras, film, supplies, and b/w film developing. 1–2 hour film developing available. This is where I have gone for 9 years, and am always satisfied.

GYMS

BFF Gym- Be Fit Forever
Ave 5 Bis & Calle 15 (Xelha)
987-120-1215
Mon - Fri: 7:00 am - 9:30 am & 5:00 pm - 9:00 pm
Sat: 7:00 am - 9:30 am

Cozumel's first all-female gym recently opened in April 2011. It is fully air conditioned, offers hydraulic equipment, cardio equipment, trainers lockers and showers. The gym is based on a Curves circuit system, meaning every single resistance machine works every major muscle group, two muscles at a time.

EGO Gym
Calle 11 # 100 Between Ave 5&10
987- 872- 4897
Monday - Friday 5am- 11pm, Saturday 6am- 6pm

This is an air conditioned gym. They offer a full service gym facility with free-weights, state of the art weight machines, cardio bikes, and stair climbers. Personal training is available. Classes offered include Pilates, spinning, yoga and kick-boxing

Muscle & Fitness Gym
Ave 55 between 5 and Hidalgo
Monday–Friday 6:30AM to 11:00PM, Saturdays 7:00 AM–9:00PM,
Sundays 9:00AM–1:00PM

Muscle and Fitness is clean, cool and spacious, with a friendly staff. The monthly fee for using the gym facilities is 200 pesos. For an additional 50 pesos you can also participate in their aerobics classes.

Studio 65 Gym & Fitness Center
Calle 7 & Ave 65 Bis
987-869-2805
Monday-Friday 6am-10pm, Saturday 8am-6pm

Studio 65 offers a full service gym facility with free-weights, state of the art weight machines, cardio bikes, and stair climbers. This is the place to go if you are serious about your fitness. Personal training is also available. Day passes for $5 USD and monthly $30. Power Yoga Cozumel is now located on the 2ND floor of the gym and offers daily power vinyasa yoga classes. Drop in students welcome! Classes separate cost from gym membership.

Unidad Deportiva Weight Lifting
Sports Park on Calle 11 between Ave 35&50

Open area with free weights, benches and other lifting equipment. If you can take the heat and humidity it is free to the public.

CHAPTER XI

COMMUNITY SERVICE

Open your heart and become a part of
Cozumel.

PEOPLE HELPING PEOPLE—COZUMEL COMMUNITY SERVICES

Those of us who are frequent visitors to Cozumel are very aware of all the organizations that serve the local population, which includes the Mexicans and those who have moved there from other countries. In the USA there are government funds and corporate fundraisers who help to finance charities. That option is usually not available in Mexico. There is so much that visitors can do to help, sometimes without spending a dime, maybe just an hour of your time. Please read this chapter and keep all of those listed in mind. From the bottom of my heart, I THANK YOU.

AMERICAN COMMUNITY SERVICES/ACS
www.cozumelinsider.com/acs

ACS is a non-profit service to benefit the residents of Cozumel. They have 2 primary objectives.

1. To benefit the community by promoting and facilitating volunteerism and philanthropist activities.

2. To enhance the knowledge and experience of Americans in Cozumel by providing information and referral services for vacations, relocations. And working and living in Cozumel.

PROJECTS SPONSORED BY ACS

BLOOD DONOR DRIVE: In conjunction with the community blood bank they are working in 3 areas to benefit all of Cozumel.

1. To establish viable donor registry comprised of both Amer4ican and Mexican residents that can be accessed 24/7 in emergencies.

2. Identify a pool of potential donors who will be available when the blood bank has a specific need.

3. Work with the medical community to launch a campaign to educate the local residents about the need for donors, and to dispel the myths about donating blood.
COZUMEL CLEAN PROJECT

This is a trash pickup project comprising a group of the local children. They work together to clean up and keep clean their neighborhoods. ACS volunteers coordinate the children's efforts. If you are on the Isle when one of these days are scheduled, come out and help. Supplies are always needed: trash bags, surgical gloves, cotton gloves. All can be dropped off at the ACS office located at 602B Melger, next to the Navy base.

MARINE TURTLE SALVATION PROJECT

A partnership with the Municipio de Cozumel to save the sea turtles from extinction. For hundreds of years turtle meat was a staple of the Mayan diet. The younger generations must be educated and strong efforts made to protect these turtles before they are gone forever. Currently there are 2 programs in operation.

1. The Parks and Museum Foundation's Punta Sur Park Salvation program is a for profit program which offers tickets @ $40 for excursion to view the turtles.

2. The City of San Miguel's volunteer salvation program covers the beaches from Mezcilito's to Punta Sur Park entrance. The city depends on volunteers, police, and the armed forces assistance on the east side of the island, during nesting season. Volunteers do most of the nightly work. Cash contributions are not usually accepted, but contributions of supplies are always welcome and sorely needed. Low level flashlights, infrared lights, batteries, 2 way radios, latex gloves, pens, water proof markers, and gas vouchers are always needed.
Read more about these projects and the effect the recent hurricane Emily has had @ www.cozumelinsider.com/turtles

CHRYSALIS

www.barefootincozumel.com/chrys.htm cozkids@hotmail.com

Chrysalis is solely dedicated to helping the children of Cozumel who are in need, to achieve their full potentials. This special program owns a large part of my heart and a percentage of any proceeds from this travel guide will be donated to Chrysalis to assist in furthering the education of these children.
Education in Mexico is not free, nor is it inexpensive for the needier families in Cozumel. Many children are deprived an education, as their families are unable to afford the costs associated with sending them to school. Registration fees, required uniforms, textbooks and school supplies can amount to one or two months of a family's total income.

The Cozumel Chrysalis Group assists financially those children who show a desire for education but are unable to attend due to the expense involved.

Chrysalis began in 1995 by a small group of expatriate ladies who wanted to "DO SOMETHING". In the first year 10 students were assisted to attend school, in 2005 there are over 250 who are able to attend school due to the efforts of this group. This group is pure Non-profit, absolutely NO ONE is in a paid position. Every one that gives of themselves and their time, does so for free and for the love and appreciation of these children. HOW TO HELP!

Sponsorship: A one-time donation of $80 U.S. for elementary students child's education. If you are unable to donate this much, consider a
small cash/check, even $5 will help.

Used clothing sale: Bring good/clean used clothing in your luggageeach trip. These are sold at yard sales and helps families two ways. They are able to buy good clothing for a few pesos, and then those pesos add up and are used for purchasing uniforms and supplies. Used clothing, school supplies and financial donations may be dropped off at one of three locations: Tony Rome's Restaurant on 5 Ave between
Salas and Calle 3, Hotel Aguilar on Calle 3 and 5 Ave, or at Paradise Beach School supplies: Check the web site for current needs, but usually pens, markers, book bags, calculators are on the list. Check first for specifics.

Carnaval Booth: This project is a big fundraiser for Chrysalis. A booth is set up during Carnaval and beads, masks, and other carnaval trinkets are sold, or games are played. Donate your throw beads from Mardi Gras, purchase a few novelty beads and bring them, the same with masks. Offer to carry some of our purchased supplies over on your trip. If you will be here during Carnaval, offer to work a shift at the booth. You will make new friends, helping the children, and have a load of fun.

Whatever you do, do something. Every little bit helps. Look at your own children and grandchildren and think how terrible it would be if they were unable to get any education. THANK YOU.

CORAL PARK BUDDY PROGRAM

A fund raising program to save the reefs of Cozumel. Make a donation at www. coralreefalliance.org/divein/parkbuddy
Or go to the site to read about the projects underway to protect and save the reefs. Contact is Eileen Weckerle @ eweckerle@coral.

FRIENDS OF CRUZ ROJA
Cruz Roja Cozumel (Cozumel Red Cross)
www.cruzrojacozumel.org
cozredcross@earthlink.net

Cruz Roja Cozumel, the Cozumel Red Cross, provides vital services to maintain health and safety for all of the island's residents and visitors. We serve the community 24/ free ambulances in cases of emergency, free and low-cost medical services; lifeguard, first aid and other training; health education and disaster preparation and relief.

The «Friends» is comprised of tourists, vacation-home owners, divers, cruisers and ex-pats united by a desire to support the warm and hospitable people who make this island so wonderful.

There are many ways you can help this wonderful organization. I will briefly review them but please go to the website and read more. Money! It is always welcome and it is used for supplies purchased in the USA, as it buys a lot more there than in Cozumel.

Network; ask your doctor, dentist, anyone medically connected If they have access to discounts on supplies, even better, do they have some to donate.

Be a mule, let Cruz Roja have supplies mailed to you so that you can carry it over in your suitcase. Just send an email with your dates and how much room you can spare.

Your time, offer to volunteer or attend our golf and casino night fundraisers, help us at community events such as the Cozumel Ironman and our Carnval booth in the Plaza, or assist with collections if you will be here.

On your departure from Cozumel airport, drop off your unused pesos into one of the Cruz Roja boxes at the airport.

DIVE WITH MARTIN DONATIONS: Accepts used prescription glasses and hearing aids. He will reward you with a free dive for 2 pairs of glasses or 1 hearing aide. Email DWM@prodigy.net.mx

FRIENDS OF COZUMEL
www.friendsofcozumel.com
Karen@friendsofcozumel.com

Friends of Cozumel is an informal network of families, friends, colleagues, donors and volunteers who share a common interest in benefitting families in need as well as the broader community of Cozumel, Mexico.

Our goal is to help families and organizations become self-sufficient and to improve their quality of life and to work alongside us to help others. Our focus is connecting people and resources to :

• Promote volunteerism and develop local leadership skills
• Support education and learning for youth and adults.We strongly believe in providing developmental opportunities so people learn to help themselves.
• Benefit families and individuals who need assistance
• Benefit the community by sponsoring projects related to the environment, health and safety, culture, etc.

We welcome support from visitors, island residents, and those who want to help from their home location. You can get involved in the following ways:

• Volunteer for a one-time event or on an ongoing basis. We can help identify volunteer needs on the island that fit your interests and time available.

• Help with a specific project (i.e. school supplies to support education for children); an educational opportunity (i.e. practice conversational English or job skills classes for women); or Christian education (i.e. Bible School youth program)

• Provide one-time or ongoing support as a volunteer or donor for a specific family in need (i.e. food, clothing) or a local non-profit organization (i.e. provide facility maintenance support, teach a class)

• Participate as a Mission volunteer for 1-7 days. Mission Project weeks are scheduled twice a year. Island residents and visitors can participate part-time or full-time during these weeks. Mission projects focus on Christian ministry, children and families in need, education, and children with disabilities.

Skills needed included construction, repairs, painting; teaching, education, communication, crafts/sewing, art/design; music; bilingual Spanish-English translation; writing, public relations, photography; problem solving and organizational capabilities, etc.

• Volunteer as a «super shopper» to purchase new or collect gently used in-kind donations in your home location (i.e. school supplies, clothing, mission project supplies)

• Transport donations to Cozumel if you are traveling via airline or cruise ship.

• Donate cash or in-kind contributions of items or services. Wish Lists of needs are identified with community leaders and updated quarterly. Go to www. friendsofcozumel.com/your help/wishlists/

• Connect us to organizations, individuals, opportunities and resources that fit with our goal of helping families and organizations become self-sufficient.

HUMANE SOCIETY OF COZUMEL
www.islecozumel.net/services/spca
011-52-987-857-0849

Founded in 1996 with a one-time grant from the government, they are now only able to continue operation with the donations and volunteer services of those who care.

SERVICES:

At cost Vet services.
Spay-neuter program.
Adoption program
Free euthanasia

There are several ways you can help this worthy organization.

1. Volunteer a few hours or a few days of your trip. Help clean up, work on repairs, or just walk and play with the animals.

2. Adopt a dog or cat to take home. The shelter will assist with arrangements.

3. Donate supplies. Always needed is medical supplies, surgical gloves, and bandages, call and ask.

4. Cash donations ALWAYS welcome.

Patricia's Humane Society adoptees, Poppy , Lobito, and cousin Cash.

Cozumel Cruz Roja (Red Cross)

CHAPTER XII

LET'S SPEAK SPANISH

Basic Spanish for vacation

You could manage quite well in Cozumel without ever speaking a word of Spanish, but please remember we are the guests. Most of the people who work in the tourist industry can speak some English and understand pretty well. But if you at least make an attempt to speak in thier language, you will not be laughed at, but receive a big smile and maybe some help with your Spanish. If you venture into some of the less touristy areas, you will find you are able to do so much more just with the basic words and phrases, so come on give it a try.

Tip: *Use sticky notes and label everything at home in Spanish, without the English, you will quickly pick up words that way.*

Basic Interactions

Hola
hi

adiós
goodbye

sí
yes

no
no

por favor
please

gracias
thanks

muchas gracias
thanks a lot

dispénseme
excuse me

perdón
pardon

OK
OK

de nada
you're welcome

hasta mañana
see you tomorrow

hasta luego
see you later

adelante
come in

siéntese
sit down

repita
say it again

traduzca
translate

señor
sir

señora
madam

señorita
miss

el amigo
the friend (male)

la amiga
the friend (female)

el esposo
the husband

la esposa
the wife

salud
cheers, gesundheit

PHRASES

¿Cómo se llama usted?
What's your name?

Me llamo (María).
My name is (Maria).

Mucho gusto.
Pleased to meet you.

¿De dónde es usted?
Where are you from?

Soy de (Nueva York).
I'm from (New York).

¿Habla inglés?
Do you speak English?

Hablo un poco de español.
I speak a little Spanish.

¿Cómo se dice…en español?
How do you say…in Spanish?

¿Qué significa…?
What does…mean?

¿Cómo se pronuncia esta palabra?
How do you pronounce this word?

el teléfono público
the public telephone

los servicios
public toilets (1)

los baños públicos
public toilets (2)

el paradero de autobuses
the bus stop

la estación del metro
the subway station

el estacionamiento
the parking garage

el museo
the museum

el semáforo
the traffic light

la farmacia
the drugstore

el mercado
the market

el poste de luz
the streetlight

la calle
the street

la policía
the police

el cruce
the intersection
el letrero
the street sign

la panadería
the bakery

la esquina
the corner

el basurero
the trash basket

el/la peatón(a)
the pedestrian

la librería
the bookstore

el taxi
the taxi cab

la avenida
the avenue

el zócalo
the main square

el quiosco de periódicos
the news stand

el supermercado
the supermarket

PHRASES

¿Dónde están los servicios higiénicos?
Where is the bathroom?

¿Dónde están los baños públicos?
Where is the bathroom?
¿Dónde está el paradero de autobuses?
Where is the bus stop?

¿Puede ayudarme?
Can you help me?

No comprendo.
I don't understand.

Me he perdido.
I'm lost.

¿Dónde está la zona comercial?
Where is the main area for shopping?

¿Hay una guía telefónica?
Is there a phone directory?

¡Socorro!
Help!

Mi dirección es…
My address is…

Hotel Spanish

el cuarto de baño

the bathroom

la cama
the bed

la pensión
the boarding house

el cuarto doble
the double room

el ascensor
the elevator
la llave
the key

la entrada
the lobby

el/la gerente
the manager

servicio de cuarto
room service

la ducha
the shower

el portero
the porter

el botones
the bellhop

el huésped
the guest

el balcón
the balcony

con aire acondicionado
air-conditioned

la bañera
the bathtub

la cuenta
the bill

el recibo
the receipt

el desayuno
the breakfast
la cena
the dinner

el almuerzo
the lunch

cuarto con desayuno
bed and breakfast

la cama matrimonial
the double bed

pensión completa
full board

media pensión
half board

PHRASES

¿Puede recomendarme un hotel barato?
Can you recommend a cheap hotel?

¿Cuánto cobra por noche?
What's the cost per nite?

¿Hay algo más barato?
Is there anything cheaper?

¿Tiene cuartos libres?
Do you have any vacancies?

Quisiera un cuarto sencillo.
I'd like a single room.

¿Me permite ver el cuarto?
May I see the room?

No hay agua caliente.
There isn't any hot water.

No me gusta esta habitación.
I don't like this room.

¿Cuánto cuesta por semana?
What's the weekly rate?

¿Están las comidas incluidas?
Are meals included?

Dining Out

la bebida
the beverage

bien cocido
well-done

la cuchara
the spoon

el cuchillo
the knife

la cuenta
the bill

la mesa
the table

el mesero/el camarero
the waiter

el menú
the menu

menú del día
set menu

el pan
bread

picante
spicy

la pimienta
the pepper

el pimentero
the pepper shaker

el platillo
the saucer

el plato
the plate

poco cocido
rare

el postre
dessert

la propina
the tip

la sal
the salt

el salero
the salt shaker

la servilleta
the napkin

la tarjeta de crédito
the credit card

la taza
the cup

el tenedor
the fork

el vaso
the glass

PHRASES

¿Qué está incluido?
What is included?

¿Viene con ensalada?
Does it come with salad?

¿Cuál es la sopa del día?
What is the soup of the day?

¿Qué me recomienda?
What do you recommend?

¿Puede darme…?
Can you bring me…?

La cuenta, por favor.
The bill, please.

Estuvo delicioso.
That was delicious.

¿Dónde hay un buen restaurante?
Where is there a good restaurant?

Quisiera reservar una mesa para dos.
I'd like to reserve a table for two.

¿Qué clase de...tiene?
What type of...do you have?

Shopping

el carrito
the shopping cart

la cesta
the basket
la carnicería
the butcher's shop

la panadería
the bakery

el quiosco
the newsstand

la tienda de modas
the clothes shop

la papelería
the stationery shop

la plaza del mercado
the marketplace

la zapatería
the shoe shop

caro(a)
expensive

barato(a)
cheap

ir de compras
to go shopping

comprar
to buy

pagar
to pay

abierto
open

cerrado
closed
cerrado al mediodía
closed for lunch

la tarjeta de crédito
the credit card

la joyería
the jewelers

la salida
the exit

la entrada
the entrance

de mejor calidad
better quality

el recibo
the receipt

defectuoso(a)
defective

roto(a)
broken

PHRASES

¿Cuánto cuesta?
How much does it cost?

Es demasiado caro.
It's too expensive.

¿Tiene algo más barato?
Do you have anything cheaper?

¿Puedo probármelo?
Can I try it on?

El color no me sienta bien.
The color doesn't suit me.

¿Dónde están los probadores?
Where are the changing rooms?

Voy a pagar al contado.
I'm going to pay cash.

¿Puede atenderme?
Can you help me?

Sólo estoy mirando.
I'm just looking.

¿Podría mostrarme…?
Could you show me…?

Medical

la medicina
the medicine

la cápsula
the capsule

la tableta
the tablet

la píldora
the pill

la inyección
the injection

el ungüento
the ointment

descanso en cama
bed rest

la cirugía
the surgery

la toalla calentadora
the heating pad

la bolsa de hielo
the ice pack

el soporte
the sling

el enyesado
the cast

la muleta
the crutch

el médico
the doctor

la enfermera
the nurse

el salpullido
the rash

los escalofríos
the chills

el dolor
the pain

alta presión sanguínea
high blood pressure

el resfriado
the cold

la torcedura
the sprain
la infección
the infection

la fractura
the broken bone

la cortada
the cut

el golpe
the bruise

PHRASES

Estoy enfermo(a).
I'm sick.

¿Dónde le duele?
Where does it hurt?

¿Tiene fiebre?
Do you have a fever?

¿Desde cuándo se siente así?
How long have you felt this way?

¿Podría llamar a un médico, por favor?
Could you please call a doctor?

¿Puede visitarme el médico?
Can the doctor come here?

Tengo náuseas
I feel nauseous.

Tengo alergia.
I have an allergy.

Tengo diarrea.
I have diarrhea

Tengo migraña.
I have a migraine.

Beach time

la playa
the beach

el mar
the sea

tomar el sol
to sunbathe

la piscina
the swimming pool

el/la salvavidas
the lifeguard

el colchón neumático
the air mattress

la sombrilla
the umbrella

la pelota de playa
the beach ball

los lentes oscuros
the sunglasses

el traje de baño
the bathing suit

la ola
the wave

nadar
to swim

la arena
the sand

el respirador
the snorkel

la crema solar
the sunblock

la concha marina
the sea shell

la nevera
the cooler

el/la bañista
the sunbather

el agua
the water

el planeador de mar
the surfboard

el planeador pequeño de agua
the kickboard

la costa
the coast

la toalla
the towel

la marea alta
the high tide

la marea baja
the low tide

PHRASES

¿Hay algún salvavidas?
Is there a lifeguard?

¿Es seguro para niños?
Is it safe for children?

¿Es seguro nadar aquí?
Is it safe to swim here?

¿Podemos nadar aquí?
Can we swim here?

¿La playa es de arena?
Is the beach sandy?

¿Se puede bucear aquí sin peligro?
Can one dive here without danger?

¿Hay una contracorriente peligrosa?
Is there a dangerous undertow?

¿A qué hora es la marea alta?
What time is high tide?

¿A qué hora es la marea baja?
What time is low tide?

¿Hay una corriente fuerte?
Is there a strong current?

Airport talk

la maleta
the suitcase

el equipaje
the baggage

el boleto
the ticket

el guardia de seguridad
the security guard

el detector de metales
the metal detector

el seleccionador de rayos
the x-ray machine

la banda
the conveyor belt

el carrito de equipaje
the baggage cart

el maletero
the porter

la sección de no fumar
the non-smoking section

el pasaporte
the passport

el talón
the baggage claim ticket

el maletín
the carry-on bag

la aduana
the customs office

el reclamo de equipaje
the baggage claim area

el pase de abordar
the boarding pass

el, la sobrecargo
the flight attendant

el compartimiento de equipaje
the luggage compartment

la mesita
the tray table

el pasillo
the aisle

la terminal
the terminal building

la pista
the runway

el vuelo
the flight

el ala
the wing

la cola
the tail

PHRASES

¿Qué terminal necesita Ud.?
What terminal do you need?

Busco la terminal norte.
I'm looking for the north terminal.

¿Para dónde sale Ud.?
Where are you headed?

Voy a México.
I'm going to Mexico.

La terminal norte es para los vuelos internacionales.
The north terminal is for international flights.

¿Dónde puedo reclamar mi equipaje?
Where can I claim my luggage?

¿Dónde está la aduana?
Where is customs?

Por favor, ¿me puede ayudar con las maletas?
Could you please help me with my bags?

¿Me permite ver su talón?
Could I see your baggage claim ticket?

¿Cuántas maletas tiene?
How many bags do you have?

Days & Months

January Enero
February Febrero
March Marzo
April Abril
May Mayo

June Junio
July Julio
August Agosto
September Septiembre
October Octubre
November Noviembre
December Diciembre

Monday Lunes
Tuesday Martes
Wednesday Miércoles
Thursday Jueves
Friday Viernes
Saturday Sábado
Sunday Domingo

Colors

White blanco
Blue azul
Red rojo
green verde
yellow amarillo
Black negro

Numbers

Zero cero
One uno
Two dos
Three tres
four cuatro
five cinco
six seis
seven siete
eight ocho
nine nueve
ten diez

eleven once
twelve doce
thirteen trece
fourteen catorce
fifteen quince
sixteen dieciséis
seventeen diecisiete
eighteen dieciocho
nineteen diecinueve
twenty veinte
thirty treinta
forty cuarenta
fifty cincuenta
sixty sesenta
seventy setenta
eighty ochenta
ninety noventa
one hundred cien
one thousand mil

CHAPTER XIII

USEFUL INTERNET SITES

Discussion board sites and lots of useful information.

DISCUSSION BOARDS AND HELPFUL
INTERNET SITES

The discussion boards listed are ones that at least read almost every day, as do many other frequent visitors and Cozumel locals. These boards are a great place to get your questions answered. Everyone is friendly and will welcome you to the discussions. I have met many of my friends on these boards and even better have met many of them in Cozumel. We often arrange parties at one of the local restaurants, where everyone who is on the Island at the same time gets together, including many of the locals. So come on, join in and make some Cozumel friends.

DISCUSSION BOARDS

BOOTS N ALL TRAVEL
www.bootsnall.com/insiders/namerica/mexico.shtrr

List of insiders from all of Mexico, willing to answer any question you might have about their area.

COZUMEL4YOU
www.czm4you.com

This is a fairly new site with lots of information. It has a discussion board frequented by locals and a weekly news letter
www.cozguide.net

Online travel guide for Cozumel and Riveria Maya. Includes a chat room and an abundance of information.

COZUMEL INSIDER
www.cozumelinsider.com

Not a discussion board, but offers a wealth of information for visitors and locals alike.

COZUMEL UNDERGROUND
http://wahootours.hyperboards2.com/index.cgi?

Forum sponsored by Jim Wilson of Wahoo Tours. Jim's daily posts of
news and Cozumel happenings are fantastic and often entertaining.
Frequented by Cozumel locals and frequent visitors to the Island, you can
definitely get your questions answered here.

MYCOZUMELCOMMUNITY
www.cozumel-hotels.net/yabbse/index.php

Yet another great forum with information related to Cozumel and more.
Moderated by Tony Rome, a twenty year resident of the Island. Have a
problem on Cozumel, CALL TONY!

TRAVEL NOTES COZUMEL
www.travelnotes.cc

Forum where you can ask question or just visit with Cozumel locals
and visitors. Links to tours, hotels, dining, and lots of reviews.

SCUBA BOARD
www.scubaboard.com

Has a forum specific to diving in Cozumel. Great place to inquire about
dive operators etc.

THE GRINGO GUIDE
www.gringoguide.com

Cozumel forum and trip reports.

OTHER USEFUL SITES

OFFICIAL COZUMEL SITE
http://www.islacozumel.com.mx/homeing.asp

Official government welcome to Cozumel.

Cozumel-Cancun Travel
http://home.pcisys.net/~ronlee/Scuba/Cozumel/Aug2001/CancunCozumel.htm
Great in depth information on the Riveria Bus for travel between
Cancun and Cozumel.

Cedral Homes
http://www.cedral.net/

Builder's site with information about building a home on Cozumel.

Playa del Carmen Transportation
http://www.entertainment-plus.net/tour_tpt_pdc.cfm

Van transportation between Cancun Airport and Playa del Carmen.

Cancún Travel
http://www.cancuntravel.com/transfers.asp

More van options from Cancun

Seat Guru. Com
http://www.seatguru.com

Cool site for picking the best seats on air craft and avoiding the bad.

Metric Conversions
http://www.sciencemadesimple.net/conversions.html

Great site for converting those metric measures into something familiar
to us Americans.

ATM Locator
http://visa.via.infonow.net/locator/global/jsp/SearchPage.jsp

Locate ATMs anywhere in the world.

Map Chick
http://www.mapchick.com

Offers a great mini guide to Cozumel on a map. You will be surprised
how much is on there. A must have.

Currency Converter
http://www.xe.com/ucc

Offers up to date currency conversion. Put the amount in and convert.

Translation Service
http://www.freetranslation.com

Offers free translation online.

Trip Advisor
http://www.tripadvisor.com

Find reviews on Hotels and more.

LAST MINUTE TIPS
BEFORE YOU GO!

#1 TIP: "Travel with an open mind; be thrilled, not provoked, with things that are different." Harvey S. Olson, chairman of Olson-Travel World Organization

If you do not like hard beds bring a mattress pad or foam pad with you. Most beds in Cozumel are on platforms of some kind and they are extremely firm.

Toilet paper is not always available in rest rooms; bring tissues and wet wipes to keep with you.

Bring scented candles or air freshener. At some times of the year rooms have a very musty smell, due to the humidity?

Don't forget the bug spray, also try some bounce softener sheets tucked into your blouse or shirt, the mosquitoes do not like it and stay away.

Make copies of your passport, birth certificate, and important papers to keep in your wallet. Lock up the real stuff.

Drop off your laundry for washing the day before you leave the Island, and go home with clean cloths.
Bring large re-sealable plastic bags for those last minute wet bathing suits and wet suits.

The Electricity in Mexico is 110 Volt, 60 cycles, like the USA. It may be a problem to find the modern three prong outlets in some places, so you may need a two/three prong adapter.

Tap water should be considered unsafe. Bottled water and purification tablets or drops are cheap and readily available. Restaurants only use purified water, so they are safe. Get in the habit of not using tap water to rinse your mouth when brushing teeth; close your mouth in the shower To clarify this, I have used tap to brush my teeth for years, but this is a popular warning out there.

You can take the sting out of that sunburn by dabbing or spraying on white distilled vinegar after a cool shower. It really works! You may smell like a lovely tossed salad for a while, but a small price to pay for relief.

Always keep some loose change or small bills in your pocket—you never know when you're going to need some for a tip.

If you do not speak Spanish, bring a small notebook or calculator for writing prices when negotiating.

Consider bringing Pepto Bismal. I have heard that taking Pepto Bismal twice or four times a day keeps most people from getting Montezuma's Revenge. Not overdoing the tequila will probably work as well!

Keep essentials, such as a change of clothing, in your carry-on bag. Lost luggage is a fact of travel life and locating lost bags takes an average of three days. I know about this, I once wore the same outfit 3 nights in a row.

A few things that are nice to bring with you are a fold up cooler, insulated drinking cup, cork screw and bottle opener, extra film and batteries

You can buy lottery tickets in Cozumel. It's fun and could extend your vacation if you are lucky. I buy mine at the Mercado at the newspaper stand.

Cozumel's Magic Sunse

SAVE MONEY!

COZUMEL THE COMPLETE GUIDE II

COUPONS

Contact information:

www.cozumelthecompleteguide.com

cozumelcomplete2@aol.com

Find us on Facebook under Cozumel the Complete Guide

RENTADORA ISIS

011-52-987-872-3367

www.islacozumel.net/services/isis

rentadoraisis@prodigy.net.mx

Downtown Ave 5 between Calle 2&4

RECIEVE 10% OFF YOUR
RENTAL WHEN PRESENTING
THIS COUPON!

COZUMEL THE COMPLETE
GUIDE II

BOB"S COZUMEL

987-113-8678

www.facebook.com/BOBsCozumel

On the Square directly down from the ferry
just past 5th Ave on the left side

RECEIVE A FREE SOUVENIR SHOT
GLASS OF YOUR CHOICE WITH
ANY PURCHASE!

COZUMEL THE COMPLETE
GUIDE II

LA CALETA DEL TIO JOSE

987-869-0124

Carretera Costera Sur Km 2.3

Near the light house south of town.

11:00 am – 8:30 pm

GET YOUR FIRST MARGARITA
FREE WHEN PRESENTING THIS
COUPON!

COZUMEL THE COMPLETE
GUIDE

LA HACH

987-869-8403

Melgar across from Villa Blanca
Present our coupon and receive 15% off
your bill. Not available during happy
hours; 11-1 & 5-7

COZUMEL THE COMPLETE
GUIDE

COZUMEL THE COMPLETE GUIDE II

COZUMEL THE COMPLETE GUIDE II

COZUMEL THE COMPLETE GUIDE II

COZUMEL THE COMPLETE GUIDE II

LA HERRADURA
987-872-7754
Ave 30 between Calle 17 & 19
12pm-5pm and 7pm-11pm

15% 7pm to 11 pm

COZUMEL THE COMPLETE
GUIDE II

ESPECIAS
987-876-1558
Calle 3 between Ave 5 & 10
Dinner only

Free Appetizer

COZUMEL THE COMPLETE
GUIDE II

KELLEY'S BAR & GRILL
kelleysbarandgrill@yahoo.com
Ave 10 between Calle 1 & Salas

Gene Will buy your first Cerveza
or margarita with coupon!

COZUMEL THE COMPLETE
GUIDE II

KINTA
www.kintacozumel.com
987-869-0544
Ave 5between Calle 2 & 4

Enjoy free Sangria with coupon

COZUMEL THE COMPLETE
GUIDE II

**COZUMEL THE
COMPLETE
GUIDE II**

**COZUMEL THE
COMPLETE
GUIDE II**

**COZUMEL THE
COMPLETE
GUIDE II**

**COZUMEL THE
COMPLETE
GUIDE II**

KONDESA
987-869-1086
Ave 5 between Calles 5 & 7

Have a glass of their tasty
Sangria free with coupon.

COZUMEL THE COMPLETE
GUIDE II

PRIMA'S TRATTORIA
www.primacozumel.com
Melgar across from Palacio
987-872-6567

Albert is offering our readers a 10%
discount with coupon on lunch and
dinner; holidays excluded.

COZUMEL THE COMPLETE
GUIDE II

PEPE'S GRILL
www.pepesgrillcozumel.com
Melgar & Salas
987-872-0213

COZUMEL THE COMPLETE
GUIDE II

PALMERA'S
Melgar in front of ferry pier
987-872-0532

COZUMEL THE COMPLETE
GUIDE II

COZUMEL THE
COMPLETE
GUIDE II

COZUMEL THE
COMPLETE
GUIDE II

COZUMEL THE
COMPLETE
GUIDE II

COZUMEL THE
COMPLETE
GUIDE II

Two D's Diving and Tour
Adventures Calle
www.2dsdivingandtours.com

011 52 987 - 120 0730

10% discount with our coupon on
scuba diving, snorkeling tour,
private and customized tours.

The Caribbean Bol
13 between Ave 5 & Gonzalo Guerrero
staceydianne@yahoo.com

011-52-987-878-4321

Bring in our coupon and get a
free game!!!

TONY

ROME'S

10% OFF

WITH

COUPON

BETWEEN

SALAS & 3

LOS CINCO SOLES

MELGAR & CALLE 8

www.loscincosoles.com

LOS CINCO SOLES offers you

a 10% discount on your purchase

when presenting this coupon.

COZUMEL THE COMPLETE GUIDE II

COZUMEL THE COMPLETE GUIDE II

COZUMEL THE COMPLETE GUIDE II

COZUMEL THE COMPLETE GUIDE II

Cozumel Bar Hop

www.cozumelbarhop.com

011-52-987-872-2294

Get a FREE "Cozumel Bar Hop" tee shirt with coupon!

COZUMEL THE COMPLETE
GUIDE II

Cozumel Kiteboarding

cozumelkiteboarding.com

info@cozumelkiteboarding.com

adrian@cozumelkiteboarding.com

Purchase a Kiteboard from Puro Mar Surf-Kite-Bikini Shop and get a

FREE LESSON

COZUMEL THE COMPLETE
GUIDE II

FLY HIGH ADVENTURES

www.cozumelflyhighadventures.com

5 minutes South of International pier
FREE SOFT DRINK WITH TOUR

COZUMEL THE COMPLETE
GUIDE II

Paco's Kiteboarding

www.pacoskiteboarding.com

surfpacos@hotmail.com

011-52-1-987-101-5512

15% OFF INSTRUCTION

10% OFF TOURS

COZUMEL THE COMPLETE
GUIDE II

COZUMEL THE COMPLETE GUIDE II

COZUMEL THE COMPLETE GUIDE II

COZUMEL THE COMPLETE GUIDE II

COZUMEL THE COMPLETE GUIDE II

Casino Club 21

Calle 7# 398 between Ave 20 & 25

Open 11AM-3AM, 7 days/wk.

FREE 2 drinks with any play!

COZUMEL THE COMPLETE
GUIDE II

BAREFOOT IN COZUMEL

www.barefootincozumel.com

011-52-987-878-4662

10% DISCOUNT WITH COUPON

COZUMEL THE COMPLETE
GUIDE II

SPA Del SOL

CALLE 5 #34, MELGER & AVE 5

www.spadelsolcozumel.com

15% off on any treatment
except packages with coupon!

COZUMEL THE COMPLETE
GUIDE II

Have a great vacation!!!!

COZUMEL THE
COMPLETE
GUIDE II

COZUMEL THE
COMPLETE
GUIDE II

COZUMEL THE
COMPLETE
GUIDE II

COZUMEL THE
COMPLETE
GUIDE II

COZUMEL

Este libro terminó de imprimirse en noviembre de 2011
en los talleres de Grupo Impresor Unicornio S.A. de C.V.
calle 41 No. 506 x 60 y 62 Centro, C.P. 97000
Mérida, Yucatán, México.